Travel phrasebooks collection
«Everything Will Be Okay!»

T&P Books Publishing

PHRASEBOOK
ARABIC

THE MOST IMPORTANT PHRASES

This phrasebook contains the most important phrases and questions for basic communication Everything you need to survive overseas

By Andrey Taranov

T&P BOOKS

Phrasebook + 1500-word dictionary

English-Egyptian Arabic phrasebook & concise dictionary

By Andrey Taranov

The collection of "Everything Will Be Okay" travel phrasebooks published by T&P Books is designed for people traveling abroad for tourism and business. The phrasebooks contain what matters most - the essentials for basic communication. This is an indispensable set of phrases to "survive" while abroad.

Another section of the book also provides a small dictionary with more than 1,500 useful words arranged alphabetically. The dictionary includes a lot of gastronomic terms and will be helpful when ordering food at a restaurant or buying groceries at the store.

T&P Books Publishing
www.tpbooks.com

ISBN: 978-1-78716-928-9

This book is also available in E-book formats.
Please visit www.tpbooks.com or the major online bookstores.

FOREWORD

The collection of "Everything Will Be Okay" travel phrasebooks published by T&P Books is designed for people traveling abroad for tourism and business. The phrasebooks contain what matters most - the essentials for basic communication. This is an indispensable set of phrases to "survive" while abroad.

This phrasebook will help you in most cases where you need to ask something, get directions, find out how much something costs, etc. It can also resolve difficult communication situations where gestures just won't help.

This book contains a lot of phrases that have been grouped according to the most relevant topics. A separate section of the book also provides a small dictionary with more than 1,500 important and useful words.

Take "Everything Will Be Okay" phrasebook with you on the road and you'll have an irreplaceable traveling companion who will help you find your way out of any situation and teach you to not fear speaking with foreigners.

TABLE OF CONTENTS

PRONUNCIATION

T&P phonetic alphabet	Egyptian Arabic example	English example
[a]	[ṭaffa] طفّى	shorter than in ask
[ā]	[exṭār] إختار	calf, palm
[e]	[setta] ستّة	elm, medal
[i]	[minā'] ميناء	shorter than in feet
[ī]	[ebrīl] إبريل	feet, meter
[o]	[oɣosṭos] أغسطس	pod, John
[ō]	[ḥalazōn] حلزون	fall, bomb
[u]	[kalkutta] كلكتا	book
[ū]	[gamūs] جاموس	fuel, tuna
[b]	[bedāya] بداية	baby, book
[d]	[sa'āda] سعادة	day, doctor
[ḍ]	[waḍ'] وضع	[d] pharyngeal
[ʒ]	[arʒantīn] الأرجنتين	forge, pleasure
[ẓ]	[ẓahar] ظهر	[z] pharyngeal
[f]	[xafīf] خفيف	face, food
[g]	[bahga] بهجة	game, gold
[h]	[ettegāh] إتّجاه	home, have
[ḥ]	[ḥabb] حبّ	[h] pharyngeal
[y]	[dahaby] ذهبي	yes, New York
[k]	[korsy] كرسي	clock, kiss
[l]	[lammaḥ] لمّح	lace, people
[m]	[marṣad] مرصد	magic, milk
[n]	[ganūb] جنوب	sang, thing
[p]	[kaputʃino] كابتشينو	pencil, private
[q]	[wasaq] وثق	king, club
[r]	[roḥe] روح	rice, radio
[s]	[soxreya] سخرية	city, boss
[ṣ]	[me'ṣam] معصم	[s] pharyngeal
[ʃ]	['aʃā'] عشاء	machine, shark
[t]	[tanūb] تنوب	tourist, trip
[ṭ]	[xarīṭa] خريطة	[t] pharyngeal
[θ]	[mamūθ] ماموث	month, tooth
[v]	[vietnām] فيتنام	very, river
[w]	[wadda'] ودّع	vase, winter
[x]	[baxīl] بخيل	as in Scots 'loch'
[ɣ]	[etɣadda] إتغدّى	between [g] and [h]

T&P phonetic alphabet	Egyptian Arabic example	English example
[z]	[me'za] معزة	zebra, please
['] (ayn)	[sab'a] سبعة	voiced pharyngeal fricative
['] (hamza)	[sa'al] سأل	glottal stop

LIST OF ABBREVIATIONS

Egyptian Arabic abbreviations

du	-	plural noun (double)
f	-	feminine noun
m	-	masculine noun
pl	-	plural

English abbreviations

ab.	-	about
adj	-	adjective
adv	-	adverb
anim.	-	animate
as adj	-	attributive noun used as adjective
e.g.	-	for example
etc.	-	et cetera
fam.	-	familiar
fem.	-	feminine
form.	-	formal
inanim.	-	inanimate
masc.	-	masculine
math	-	mathematics
mil.	-	military
n	-	noun
pl	-	plural
pron.	-	pronoun
sb	-	somebody
sing.	-	singular
sth	-	something
v aux	-	auxiliary verb
vi	-	intransitive verb
vi, vt	-	intransitive, transitive verb
vt	-	transitive verb

ARABIC PHRASEBOOK

This section contains important phrases that may come in handy in various real-life situations.
The phrasebook will help you ask for directions, clarify a price, buy tickets, and order food at a restaurant

T&P Books Publishing

PHRASEBOOK CONTENTS

The bare minimum

Excuse me, ...	law samaḥt, ... لو سمحت، ...
Hello.	as salāmu ʿalaykum السلام عليكم
Thank you.	ʃukran شكرا
Good bye.	maʿ as salāma مع السلامة
Yes.	naʿam نعم
No.	la لا
I don't know.	la aʿrif لا أعرف
Where? | Where to? | When?	ayna? | ila ayna? | mata? أين؟ ا إلى أين؟ ا متى؟

I need ...	ana aḥtāʒ ila ... أنا أحتاج إلى...
I want ...	ana urīd ... أنا أريد ...
Do you have ...?	hal ʿindak ...? هل عندك... ؟
Is there a ... here?	hal yūʒad huna ...? هل يوجد هنا ...؟
May I ...?	hal yumkinuni ...? هل يمكنني...؟
..., please (polite request)	... min faḍlak من فضلك ...

I'm looking for ...	abḥaθ ʿan ... أبحث عن ...
restroom	ḥammām حمام
ATM	mākīnat ṣarrāf ʾāliy ماكينة صراف آلي
pharmacy (drugstore)	ṣaydaliyya صيدلية
hospital	mustaʃfa مستشفى
police station	qism aʃ ʃurṭa قسم شرطة
subway	mitru al anfāq مترو الأنفاق

taxi	taksi **تاكسي**
train station	mahattat al qiṭār **محطة القطار**

My name is ...	ismi ... **إسمي...**
What's your name?	ma smuka? **ما اسمك؟**
Could you please help me?	sā'idni min fadlak **ساعدني من فضلك**
I've got a problem.	'indi muʃkila **عندي مشكلة**
I don't feel well.	la aʃ'ur bi χayr **لا أشعر بخير**
Call an ambulance!	ittaṣil bil is'āf! **إتصل بالإسعاف!**
May I make a call?	hal yumkinuni iʒrā' mukālama tilifūniyya? **هل يمكنني إجراء مكالمة هاتفية؟**

I'm sorry.	ana 'āṣif **أنا آسف**
You're welcome.	al 'afw **العفو**

I, me	ana **أنا**
you (inform.)	anta **أنت**
he	huwa **هو**
she	hiya **هي**
they (masc.)	hum **هم**
they (fem.)	hum **هم**
we	nahnu **نحن**
you (pl)	antum **أنتم**
you (sg, form.)	hadritak **حضرتك**

ENTRANCE	duχūl **دخول**
EXIT	χurūʒ **خروج**
OUT OF ORDER	mu'aṭṭal **معطل**
CLOSED	muɣlaq **مغلق**

OPEN	maftūḥ **مفتوح**
FOR WOMEN	lis sayyidāt **للسيدات**
FOR MEN	lir riʒāl **للرجال**

Questions

Where?	ayna? أين؟
Where to?	ila ayna? إلى أين؟
Where from?	min ayna? من أين؟
Why?	limāða? لماذا؟
For what reason?	li ayy sabab? لأي سبب؟
When?	mata? متى؟
How long?	kam waqt? كم وقتا؟
At what time?	fi ayy sā'a? في أي ساعة؟
How much?	bikam? بكم؟
Do you have …?	hal 'indak …? هل عندك …؟
Where is …?	ayna …? أين …؟
What time is it?	as sā'a kam? الساعة كم؟
May I make a call?	hal yumkinuni iʒrā' mukālama tilifūniyya? هل يمكنني إجراء مكالمة هاتفية؟
Who's there?	man hunāk? من هناك؟
Can I smoke here?	hal yumkinuni at tadχīn huna? هل يمكنني التدخين هنا؟
May I …?	hal yumkinuni …? هل يمكنني …؟

Needs

I'd like ...	urīd an ... أريد أن...
I don't want ...	la urīd an ... لا أريد أن...
I'm thirsty.	ana ʿatʃān أنا عطشان
I want to sleep.	urīd an anām أريد أن أنام
I want ...	urīd an ... أريد أن...
to wash up	aɣtasil أغتسل
to brush my teeth	unazzif asnāni أنظف أسناني
to rest a while	astarīḥ qalīlan أستريح قليلا
to change my clothes	uɣayyir malābisi أغير ملابسي
to go back to the hotel	arʒiʿ ilal funduq أرجع إلى الفندق
to buy ...	aʃtari ... أشتري ...
to go to ...	aðhab ila ... أذهب إلى ...
to visit ...	azūr ... أزور ...
to meet with ...	uqābil ... أقابل ...
to make a call	uʒri mukālama hātifiyya أجري مكالمة هاتفية
I'm tired.	ana taʿibt أنا تعبت
We are tired.	naḥnu taʿibna نحن تعبنا
I'm cold.	ana bardān أنا بردان
I'm hot.	ana ḥarrān أنا حران
I'm OK.	ana bi χayr أنا بخير

I need to make a call.	aḥtāʒ ila iʒrā' mukālama hātifiyya **أحتاج إلى إجراء مكالمة هاتفية**
I need to go to the restroom.	aḥtāʒ ila ḥammām **أحتاج إلى حمام**
I have to go.	yaʒib 'alayya an aðhab **يجب علي أن أذهب**
I have to go now.	yaʒib 'alayya an aðhab al 'ān **يجب علي أن أذهب الآن**

Asking for directions

Excuse me, ...	law samaḥt, ... **لو سمحت، ...**
Where is ...?	ayna ...? **أين ...؟**
Which way is ...?	ayna aṭ ṭarīq ila ...? **أين الطريق إلى ...؟**
Could you help me, please?	hal yumkinak musāʿadati, min faḍlak? **هل يمكنك مساعدتي، من فضلك؟**
I'm looking for ...	abḥaθ ʿan ... **أبحث عن ...**
I'm looking for the exit.	abḥaθ ʿan ṭarīq al χurūʒ **أبحث عن طريق الخروج**
I'm going to ...	ana ðāhib ila... **أنا ذاهب إلى...**
Am I going the right way to ...?	hal ana ʿalaṭ ṭarīq as ṣaḥīḥ ila ...? **هل أنا على الطريق الصحيح إلى... ؟**
Is it far?	hal huwa baʿīd? **هل هو بعيد؟**
Can I get there on foot?	hal yumkinuni an aṣil ila hunāk māʃiyan? **هل يمكنني أن أصل إلى هناك ماشيا؟**
Can you show me on the map?	arīni ʿalal χarīṭa min faḍlak **أريني على الخريطة من فضلك**
Show me where we are right now.	arīni naḥnu ayna al ʾān **أريني أين نحن الآن**
Here	huna **هنا**
There	hunāk **هناك**
This way	min huna **من هنا**
Turn right.	inʿaṭif yamīnan **إنعطف يمينا**
Turn left.	inʿaṭif yasāran **إنعطف يسارا**
first (second, third) turn	awwal (θāni, θāliθ) ʃāriʿ **أول (ثاني، ثالث) شارع**

to the right	ilal yamīn **إلى اليمين**
to the left	ilal yasār **إلى اليسار**
Go straight ahead.	iðhab ilal amām mubāʃaratan **إذهب إلى أمام مباشرة**

Signs

WELCOME!	marḥaban **مرحبا**
ENTRANCE	duχūl **دخول**
EXIT	χurūʒ **خروج**
PUSH	idfa' **إدفع**
PULL	isḥab **إسحب**
OPEN	maftūḥ **مفتوح**
CLOSED	muɣlaq **مغلق**
FOR WOMEN	lis sayyidāt **للسيدات**
FOR MEN	lir riʒāl **للرجال**
GENTLEMEN, GENTS (m)	ar riʒāl **الرجال**
WOMEN (f)	as sayyidāt **السيدات**
DISCOUNTS	taχfīḍāt **تخفيضات**
SALE	'ūkazyūn **أوكازيون**
FREE	maʒʒānan **مجانا**
NEW!	ʒadīd! **جديد!**
ATTENTION!	intabih! **إنتبه!**
NO VACANCIES	la tūʒad ɣuraf χāliya **لا توجد غرف خالية**
RESERVED	maḥʒūz **محجوز**
ADMINISTRATION	al idāra **الإدارة**
STAFF ONLY	lil 'āmilīn faqaṭ **للعاملين فقط**

BEWARE OF THE DOG!	iḥtaris min al kalb! !إحترس من الكلب
NO SMOKING!	mamnūʿ at tadχīn! !ممنوع التدخين
DO NOT TOUCH!	mamnūʿ al lams! !ممنوع اللمس
DANGEROUS	χaṭīr خطير
DANGER	χaṭar خطر
HIGH VOLTAGE	ʒuhd ʿāli جهد عالي
NO SWIMMING!	mamnūʿ as sibāḥa! !ممنوع السباحة

OUT OF ORDER	muʿaṭṭal معطل
FLAMMABLE	qābil lil iʃtiʿāl قابل للإشتعال
FORBIDDEN	mamnūʿ ممنوع
NO TRESPASSING!	mamnūʿ at taʿaddi! !ممنوع التعدي
WET PAINT	ṭilāʾ ḥadīθ طلاء حديث

CLOSED FOR RENOVATIONS	muɣlaq lit taʒdīdāt مغلق للتجديدات
WORKS AHEAD	amāmak aʿmāl fiṭ ṭarīq أمامك أعمال طرق
DETOUR	taḥwīla تحويلة

Transportation. General phrases

plane	ṭā'ira **طائرة**
train	qiṭār **قطار**
bus	ḥāfila **حافلة**
ferry	safīna **سفينة**
taxi	taksi **تاكسي**
car	sayyāra **سيارة**
schedule	ʒadwal **جدول**
Where can I see the schedule?	ayna yumkinuni an ara al ʒadwal? **أين يمكنني أن أرى الجدول؟**
workdays (weekdays)	ayyām al usbū' **أيام الأسبوع**
weekends	nihāyat al usbū' **نهاية الأسبوع**
holidays	ayyām al 'uṭla ar rasmiyya **أيام العطلة الرسمية**
DEPARTURE	al muɣādara **المغادرة**
ARRIVAL	al wuṣūl **الوصول**
DELAYED	muta'aχχira **متأخرة**
CANCELLED	ulɣiyat **ألغيت**
next (train, etc.)	al qādim **القادم**
first	al awwal **الأول**
last	al aχīr **الأخير**
When is the next ...?	mata al ... al qādim? **القادم؟ ... متى الـ**
When is the first ...?	mata awwal ...? **متى أول ...؟**

When is the last ...?	mata 'āχir ...? **متى آخر ...؟**
transfer (change of trains, etc.)	taɣyīr **تغيير**
to make a transfer	uɣayyir **أغير**
Do I need to make a transfer?	hal yaʒib 'alayya taɣyīr al ...? **هل يجب علي تغيير الـ...؟**

Buying tickets

Where can I buy tickets?	ayna yumkinuni ʃirā' tazākir? أين يمكنني شراء التذاكر؟
ticket	taðkara تذكرة
to buy a ticket	ʃirā' at taðkira شراء تذكرة
ticket price	si'r at taðkira سعر التذكرة

Where to?	ila ayna? إلى أين؟
To what station?	ila ayy maḥaṭṭa? إلى أي محطة؟
I need ...	ana urīd ... أنا أريد ...
one ticket	taðkara wāḥida تذكرة واحدة
two tickets	taðkaratayn تذكرتين
three tickets	θalāθat taðākir ثلاث تذاكر

one-way	ðahāb faqaṭ ذهاب فقط
round-trip	ðahāban wa iyāban ذهابا وإيابا
first class	ad daraʒa al ūla الدرجة الأولى
second class	ad daraʒa aθ θāniya الدرجة الثانية

today	al yawm اليوم
tomorrow	ɣadan غدا
the day after tomorrow	ba'd ɣad بعد غد
in the morning	fiṣ ṣabāḥ في الصباح
in the afternoon	ba'd aẓ ẓuhr بعد الظهر
in the evening	fil masā' في المساء

aisle seat	maqʿad bi ʒānib al mamarr **مقعد بجانب الممر**
window seat	maqʿad bi ʒānib an nāfiða **مقعد بجانب النافذة**
How much?	bikam? **بكم؟**
Can I pay by credit card?	hal yumkinuni an adfaʿ bi biṭāqat iʾtimān? **هل يمكنني أن أدفع ببطاقة إئتمان؟**

Bus

bus	ḥāfila حافلة
intercity bus	ḥāfila bayn al mudun حافلة بين المدن
bus stop	maḥaṭṭat al ḥāfilāt محطة الحافلات
Where's the nearest bus stop?	ayna aqrab maḥaṭṭat al ḥāfilāt? أين أقرب محطة الحافلات؟
number (bus ~, etc.)	raqm رقم
Which bus do I take to get to …?	ayy ḥāfila ta'χuðuni ila …? أي حافلة تأخذني إلى...؟
Does this bus go to …?	hal taðhab haðihil ḥāfila ila …? هل تذهب هذه الحافلة إلى...؟
How frequent are the buses?	kam marra taðhab al ḥāfilāt? كم مرة تذهب الحافلات؟
every 15 minutes	kull χams 'aʃara daqīqa كل 15 دقيقة
every half hour	kull niṣf sā'a كل نصف ساعة
every hour	kull sā'a كل ساعة
several times a day	'iddat marrāt fil yawm عدة مرات في اليوم
… times a day	… marrāt fil yawm مرات في اليوم ...
schedule	ʒadwal جدول
Where can I see the schedule?	ayna yumkinuni an ara al ʒadwal? أين يمكنني أن أرى الجدول؟
When is the next bus?	mata al ḥāfila al qādima? متى الحافلة القادمة؟
When is the first bus?	mata awwal ḥāfila? متى أول حافلة؟
When is the last bus?	mata 'āχir ḥāfila? متى آخر حافلة؟
stop	maḥaṭṭa محطة
next stop	al maḥaṭṭa al qādima المحطة القادمة

last stop (terminus)	āχir maḥaṭṭa **آخر محطة**
Stop here, please.	qif huna min faḍlak **قف هنا من فضلك**
Excuse me, this is my stop.	law samaḥt, haðihi maḥaṭṭati **لو سمحت، هذه محطتي**

Train

train	qiṭār **قطار**
suburban train	qiṭār aḍ ḍawāḥi **قطار الضواحي**
long-distance train	qiṭār al masāfāt at ṭawīla **قطار المسافات الطويلة**
train station	maḥaṭṭat al qiṭārāt **محطة القطارات**
Excuse me, where is the exit to the platform?	law samaḥt, ayna aṭ ṭarīq ilar raṣīf **لو سمحت، أين الطريق إلى الرصيف؟**
Does this train go to ...?	ha yatawaʒʒah haðal qiṭār ila ...? **هل يتوجه هذا القطار إلى ...؟**
next train	al qiṭār al qādim **القطار القادم**
When is the next train?	mata al qiṭār al qādim? **متى القطار القادم؟**
Where can I see the schedule?	ayna yumkinuni an ara al ʒadwal? **أين يمكنني أن أرى الجدول؟**
From which platform?	min ayy raṣīf? **من أي رصيف؟**
When does the train arrive in ...?	mata yaṣil al qiṭār ila ...? **متى يصل القطار إلى... ؟**
Please help me.	sā'idni min faḍlak **ساعدني من فضلك**
I'm looking for my seat.	ana abḥaθ 'an maq'adi **أنا أبحث عن مقعدي**
We're looking for our seats.	naḥnu nabḥaθ 'an maqā'idina **نحن نبحث عن مقاعدنا**
My seat is taken.	maq'adi maʃɣūl **مقعدي مشغول**
Our seats are taken.	maqā'iduna maʃɣūla **مقاعدنا مشغولة**
I'm sorry but this is my seat.	ana 'āsif lakin haða maq'adi **أنا آسف، ولكن هذا مقعدي**
Is this seat taken?	hal haðal maq'ad maḥʒūz? **هل هذا المقعد محجوز؟**
May I sit here?	hal yumkinuni an aq'ud huna? **هل يمكنني أن أقعد هنا؟**

On the train. Dialogue (No ticket)

Ticket, please.	taðākir min faḍlak تذاكر من فضلك
I don't have a ticket.	laysat ʿindi taðkira ليست عندي تذكرة
I lost my ticket.	taðkarati ḍāʿat تذكرتي ضاعت
I forgot my ticket at home.	nasīt taðkirati fil bayt نسيت تذكرتي في البيت
You can buy a ticket from me.	yumkinak an taʃtari minni taðkira يمكنك أن تشتري مني تذكرة
You will also have to pay a fine.	kama yaʒib ʿalayk an tadfaʿ ɣarāma كما يجب عليك أن تدفع غرامة
Okay.	ḥasanan حسنا
Where are you going?	ila ayna taðhab? إلى أين تذهب؟
I'm going to ...	aðhab ila ... أذهب إلى ...
How much? I don't understand.	bikam? ana la afham بكم؟ أنا لا أفهم
Write it down, please.	uktubha min faḍlak إكتبها من فضلك
Okay. Can I pay with a credit card?	ḥasanan. hal yumkinuni an adfaʿ bi biṭāqat iʾtimān? حسنا. هل يمكنني أن أدفع ببطاقة إئتمان؟
Yes, you can.	naʿam yumkinuk نعم يمكنك
Here's your receipt.	tafaḍḍal al ʾīṣāl تفضل الإيصال
Sorry about the fine.	ʾāsif bi χuṣūṣ al ɣarāma أنا آسف بخصوص الغرامة
That's okay. It was my fault.	laysa hunāk ayy muʃkila. haðihi ɣalṭati ليس هناك أي مشكلة. هذه غلطتي
Enjoy your trip.	istamtaʿ bi riḥlatak إستمتع برحلتك

Taxi

taxi	taksi تاكسي
taxi driver	sā'iq at taksi سائق التاكسي
to catch a taxi	'āχuð taksi أخذ تاكسي
taxi stand	mawqif taksi موقف تاكسي
Where can I get a taxi?	ayna yumkinuni an 'āχuð taksi? أين يمكنني أن آخذ تاكسي؟

to call a taxi	ṭalab taksi طلب تاكسي
I need a taxi.	aḥtāʒ ila taksi أحتاج إلى تاكسي
Right now.	al 'ān الآن
What is your address (location)?	ma huwa 'unwānak? ما هو عنوانك؟
My address is ...	'unwāni fi ... عنواني في ...
Your destination?	ila ayna taðhab? إلى أين تذهب؟
Excuse me, ...	law samaḥt, ... لو سمحت، ...
Are you available?	hal anta fāḍy? هل أنت فاض؟
How much is it to get to ...?	kam adfa' li aṣil ila ...? كم أدفع لأصل إلى...؟
Do you know where it is?	hal ta'rif ayna hiya? هل تعرف أين هي؟

Airport, please.	ilal maṭār min faḍlak إلى المطار من فضلك
Stop here, please.	qif huna min faḍlak قف هنا، من فضلك
It's not here.	innaha laysat huna إنها ليست هنا
This is the wrong address.	al 'unwān χāṭi' العنوان خاطئ
Turn left.	in'aṭif ilal yasār إنعطف إلى اليسار
Turn right.	in'aṭif ilal yamīn إنعطف إلى اليمين

How much do I owe you?	kam ana mudīn lak? كم أنا مدين لك؟
I'd like a receipt, please.	aʿṭini ʾīṣāl min faḍlak. أعطني إيصالا، من فضلك.
Keep the change.	iḥtafiẓ bil bāqi إحتفظ بالباقي

Would you please wait for me?	intaẓirni min faḍlak إنتظرني من فضلك
five minutes	χams daqāʾiq خمس دقائق
ten minutes	ʿaʃar daqāʾiq عشر دقائق
fifteen minutes	rubʿ sāʿa ربع ساعة
twenty minutes	θulθ sāʿa ثلث ساعة
half an hour	niṣf sāʿa نصف ساعة

Hotel

Hello.	as salāmu 'alaykum **السلام عليكم**
My name is …	ismi … **إسمي …**
I have a reservation.	'indi ḥaʒz **لدي حجز**
I need …	urīd … **أريد …**
a single room	ɣurfa li ʃaχṣ wāḥid **غرفة لشخص واحد**
a double room	ɣurfa li ʃaχṣayn **غرفة لشخصين**
How much is that?	kam si'ruha? **كم سعرها؟**
That's a bit expensive.	hiya ɣāliya **هي غالية**
Do you have anything else?	hal 'indak χiyārāt uχra? **هل عندك خيارات أخرى؟**
I'll take it.	āχuðuha **آخذها**
I'll pay in cash.	adfa' naqdan **أدفع نقدا**
I've got a problem.	'indi muʃkila **عندي مشكلة**
My … is broken.	… mu'aṭṭal **… معطل**
My … is out of order.	… mu'aṭṭal /mu'aṭṭala/ **…معطل /معطلة/**
TV	at tilivizyūn **التليفزيون**
air conditioner	at takyīf **التكييف**
tap	al ḥanafiyya **الحنفية**
shower	ad duʃ **الدوش**
sink	al ḥawḍ **الحوض**
safe	al χazīna **الخزينة**

door lock	qifl al bāb **قفل الباب**
electrical outlet	maxraʒ al kahrabā' **مخرج الكهرباء**
hairdryer	muʒaffif aʃ ʃa'r **مجفف الشعر**

I don't have ...	laysa ladayya ... **ليس لدي ...**
water	mā' **ماء**
light	nūr **نور**
electricity	kahrabā' **كهرباء**

Can you give me ...?	hal yumkinak an ta'ṭīni ...? **هل يمكنك أن تعطيني ...؟**
a towel	fūṭa **فوطة**
a blanket	baṭṭāniyya **بطانية**
slippers	ʃabāʃib **شباشب**
a robe	rūb **روب**
shampoo	ʃambu **شامبو**
soap	ṣābūn **صابون**

I'd like to change rooms.	urīd an uɣayyir al ɣurfa **أريد أن أغير الغرفة**
I can't find my key.	la astaṭī' an aʒid miftāḥi **لا أستطيع أن أجد مفتاحي**
Could you open my room, please?	iftaḥ ɣurfati min faḍlak **إفتح غرفتي من فضلك**
Who's there?	man hunāk? **من هناك؟**
Come in!	tafaḍḍal! **تفضل!**
Just a minute!	daqīqa wāḥida! **دقيقة واحدة!**
Not right now, please.	laysa al 'ān min faḍlak **ليس الآن من فضلك**

Come to my room, please.	ta'āla ila ɣurfati law samaḥt **تعال إلى غرفتي لو سمحت**
I'd like to order food service.	urīd an yuḥḍar aṭ ṭa'ām ila ɣurfati **أريد أن يحضر الطعام إلى غرفتي**
My room number is ...	raqm gurfati huwa ... **رقم غرفتي هو ...**

I'm leaving ...	uɣādir ... **أغادر ...**
We're leaving ...	nuɣādir ... **نغادر ...**
right now	al ʾān **الآن**
this afternoon	baʿd aẓ ẓuhr **بعد الظهر**
tonight	masāʾ al yawm **مساء اليوم**
tomorrow	ɣadan **غداً**
tomorrow morning	ṣabāḥ al ɣad **صباح الغد**
tomorrow evening	masāʾ al ɣad **مساء الغد**
the day after tomorrow	baʿd ɣad **بعد غد**

I'd like to pay.	urīd an adfaʿ **أريد أن أدفع**
Everything was wonderful.	kull ʃayʾ kān rāʾiʿ **كل شيء كان رائعا**
Where can I get a taxi?	ayna yumkinuni an ʾāχuð taksi? **أين يمكنني أن آخذ تاكسي؟**
Would you call a taxi for me, please?	hal yumkinak an taṭlub li taksi law samaḥt? **هل يمكنك أن تطلب لي تاكسي لو سمحت؟**

Restaurant

Can I look at the menu, please?	hal yumkinuni an ara qā'imat aṭ ṭa'ām min faḍlak? هل يمكنني أن أرى قائمة الطعام من فضلك؟
Table for one.	mā'ida li ʃaχṣ wāḥid مائدة لشخص واحد
There are two (three, four) of us.	naḥnu iθnān (θalāθa, arba'a) نحن إثنان (ثلاثة، أربعة)
Smoking	lil mudaχχinīn للمدخنين
No smoking	li ɣayr al mudaχχinīn لغير المدخنين
Excuse me! (addressing a waiter)	law samaḥt لو سمحت
menu	qā'imat aṭ ṭa'ām قائمة الطعام
wine list	qā'imat an nabīð قائمة النبيذ
The menu, please.	al qā'ima, law samaḥt القائمة، لو سمحت
Are you ready to order?	hal anta musta'idd liṭ ṭalab? هل أنت مستعد للطلب؟
What will you have?	māða tā'χuð? ماذا تأخذ؟
I'll have ...	ana 'āhχuð ... أنا آخذ ...
I'm a vegetarian.	ana nabātiy أنا نباتي
meat	laḥm لحم
fish	samak سمك
vegetables	χuḍār خضار
Do you have vegetarian dishes?	hal 'indak aṭbāq nabātiyya? هل عندك أطباق نباتية؟
I don't eat pork.	la 'ākul al χinzīr لا آكل لحم الخنزير
He /she/ doesn't eat meat.	huwa la ya'kul /hiya la ta'kul / al laḥm هو لا يأكل /هي لا تأكل/ اللحم

I am allergic to ...	ʿindi ḥassāsiyya ḍidda ... **عندي حساسية ضد ...**
Would you please bring me ...	aḥḍir li ... min faḍlak **أحضر لي... من فضلك**
salt | pepper | sugar	milḥ | filfil | sukkar **سكر | فلفل | ملح**
coffee | tea | dessert	qahwa | ʃāy | ḥalwa **حلوى | شاي | قهوة**
water | sparkling | plain	miyāh | ɣāziyya | bidūn ɣāz **بدون غاز | غازية | مياه**
a spoon | fork | knife	milʿaqa | ʃawka | sikkīn **سكين | شوكة | ملعقة**
a plate | napkin	ṭabaq | fūṭa **فوطة| طبق**

Enjoy your meal!	bil hināʾ waʃ ʃifāʾ **بالهناء والشفاء**
One more, please.	wāḥida kamān law samaḥt **واحدة كمان من فضلك**
It was very delicious.	kānat laðīða giddan **كانت لذيذة جدا**

---

check | change | tip	ḥisāb | fakka | baqʃīʃ **بقشيش| فكة| حساب**
Check, please. (Could I have the check, please?)	aḥḍir li al ḥisāb min faḍlak? **أحضر لي الحساب من فضلك**
Can I pay by credit card?	hal yumkinuni an adfaʿ bi biṭāqat iʾtimān? **هل يمكنني أن أدفع ببطاقة إئتمان؟**
I'm sorry, there's a mistake here.	ana ʾāsif, hunāk xaṭaʾ **أنا آسف، هناك خطأ**

Shopping

Can I help you?	momken usāʿidak? هل أستطيع أن أساعدك؟
Do you have ...?	hal ʿindak ...? هل عندك ...؟
I'm looking for ...	ana abḥaθ ʿan ... أنا أبحث عن ...
I need ...	urīd ... أريد ...

I'm just looking.	ana faqat anẓur أنا فقط أنظر
We're just looking.	naḥnu faqat nanẓur نحن فقط ننظر
I'll come back later.	saʾaʿūd lāḥiqan سأعود لاحقا
We'll come back later.	sanaʿūd lāḥiqan سنعود لاحقا
discounts | sale	taɣfīḍāt | ʾūkazyūn أوكازيون تخفيضات

Would you please show me ...	arīni ... min faḍlak أريني ... من فضلك
Would you please give me ...	aʿṭini ... min faḍlak أعطني ... من فضلك
Can I try it on?	hal yumkin an uʒarribahu? هل يمكن أن أجربه؟
Excuse me, where's the fitting room?	law samaḥt, ayna ɣurfat al qiyās? لو سمحت، أين غرفة القياس؟
Which color would you like?	ayy lawn turīd? أي لون تريد؟
size | length	maqās | ṭūl طول امقاس
How does it fit?	hal yunāsibak? هل يناسبك؟

How much is it?	bikam? بكم؟
That's too expensive.	haða ɣāli ʒiddan هذا غال جدا
I'll take it.	aʃtarīhi أشتريه
Excuse me, where do I pay?	ayna yumkinuni an adfaʿ law samaḥt? أين يمكنني أن أدفع لو سمحت؟

Will you pay in cash or credit card?	hal tadfa' naqdan aw bi biṭāqat i'timān? هل تدفع نقدا أو ببطاقة إئتمان؟
In cash | with credit card	naqdan | bi biṭāqat i'timān نقدا | ببطاقة إئتمان

Do you want the receipt?	hal turīd 'īṣāl? هل تريد إيصالا؟
Yes, please.	na'am, min faḍlak نعم، من فضلك
No, it's OK.	la, laysa hunāk ayy moʃkila لا، ليس هناك أي مشكلة
Thank you. Have a nice day!	ʃukran. yawmak sa'īd شكرا. يومك سعيد

In town

Excuse me, please.	law samaḥt لو سمحت
I'm looking for ...	ana abḥaθ ʻan ... أنا أبحث عن ...
the subway	mitru al anfāq مترو الأنفاق
my hotel	funduqi فندقي
the movie theater	as sinima السينما
a taxi stand	mawqif taksi موقف تاكسي
an ATM	mākīnat ṣarrāf ʼāliy ماكينة صراف آلي
a foreign exchange office	maktab ṣarrāfa مكتب صرافة
an internet café	maqha intirnit مقهى انترنت
... street	ʃāriʻ... شارع ...
this place	haðal makān هذا المكان
Do you know where ... is?	hal taʻrif ayna ...? هل تعرف أين ...؟
Which street is this?	ma ism haðaʃ ʃāriʻ? ما اسم هذا الشارع؟
Show me where we are right now.	arīni naḥnu ayna al ʼān? أريني أين نحن الآن؟
Can I get there on foot?	hal yumkinuni an aṣil ila hunāk māʃiyan? هل يمكنني أن أصل إلى هناك ماشيا؟
Do you have a map of the city?	hal ʻindak χarīṭa lil madīna? هل عندك خريطة للمدينة؟
How much is a ticket to get in?	bikam taðkarat ad duχūl? بكم تذكرة الدخول؟
Can I take pictures here?	hal yumkinuni at taṣwīr huna? هل يمكنني التصوير هنا؟
Are you open?	hal ... maftūḥ? هل ... مفتوح؟

When do you open?	mata taftaḥūn? **متى تفتحون؟**
When do you close?	mata tuɣliqūn? **متى تغلقون؟**

Money

money	nuqūd **نقود**
cash	naqd **نقد**
paper money	'umla waraqiyya **عملة ورقية**
loose change	fakka **فكة**
check | change | tip	ḥisāb | fakka | baqʃiʃ **بقشيش| فكة| حساب**
credit card	bitāqat i'timān **بطاقة إئتمان**
wallet	maḥfaẓat nuqūd **محفظة نقود**
to buy	ʃirā' **شراء**
to pay	daf' **دفع**
fine	ɣarāma **غرامة**
free	maʒʒānan **مجانا**
Where can I buy ...?	ayna yumkinuni ʃirā' ...? **أين يمكنني شراء ...؟**
Is the bank open now?	hal al bank maftūḥ al 'ān? **هل البنك مفتوح الآن؟**
When does it open?	mata taftaḥ? **متى يفتح؟**
When does it close?	mata yuɣliq? **متى يغلق؟**
How much?	bikam? **بكم؟**
How much is this?	bikam haða? **بكم هذا؟**
That's too expensive.	haða ɣāli ʒiddan **هذا غال جدا**
Excuse me, where do I pay?	ayna yumkinuni an adfa' law samaḥt? **أين يمكنني أن أدفع لو سمحت؟**
Check, please.	al ḥisāb min faḍlak **الحساب من فضلك**

Can I pay by credit card?	hal yumkinuni an adfaʿ bi biṭāqat iʾtimān? **هل يمكنني أن أدفع ببطاقة إئتمان؟**
Is there an ATM here?	hal tūʒad huna mākīnat ṣarrāf ʾāliy? **هل توجد هنا ماكينة صراف آلي؟**
I'm looking for an ATM.	ana abḥaθ ʿan mākīnat ṣarrāf ʾāliy **أنا أبحث عن ماكينة صراف آلي**

I'm looking for a foreign exchange office.	ana abḥaθ ʿan maktab ṣarrāfa **أنا أبحث عن مكتب صرافة**
I'd like to change ...	urīd taɣyīr ... **أريد تغيير ...**
What is the exchange rate?	kam siʿr al ʿumla? **كم سعر العملة؟**
Do you need my passport?	hal taḥtāʒ ila ʒawāz safari? **هل تحتاج إلى جواز سفري؟**

Time

What time is it?	as sā'a kam? **الساعة كم؟**
When?	mata? **متى؟**
At what time?	fi ayy sā'a? **في أي ساعة؟**
now | later | after ...	al 'ān | fi waqt lāḥiq | ba'd ... **الآن | في وقت لاحق | بعد ...**
one o'clock	as sā'a al wāḥida **الساعة الواحدة**
one fifteen	as sā'a al wāḥida wa ar rub' **الساعة الواحدة والربع**
one thirty	as sā'a al wāḥida wa an niṣf **الساعة الواحدة والنصف**
one forty-five	as sā'a aθ θāniya illa rub' **الساعة الثانية إلا ربعا**
one | two | three	al wāḥida | aθ θāniya | aθ θāliθa **الواحدة | الثانية | الثالثة**
four | five | six	ar rābi'a | al χāmisa | as sādisa **الرابعة | الخامسة | السادسة**
seven | eight | nine	as sābi'a | aθ θāmina | at tāsi'a **السابعة | الثامنة | التاسعة**
ten | eleven | twelve	al 'āʃira | al ḥādiya 'aʃara | aθ θāniya 'aʃara **العاشرة | الحادية عشرة | الثانية عشرة**
in ...	ba'd ... **بعد ...**
five minutes	χams daqā'iq **خمس دقائق**
ten minutes	'aʃar daqā'iq **عشر دقائق**
fifteen minutes	rub' sā'a **ربع ساعة**
twenty minutes	θulθ sā'a **ثلث ساعة**
half an hour	niṣf sā'a **نصف ساعة**
an hour	sā'a **ساعة**

in the morning	fiṣ ṣabāḥ **في الصباح**
early in the morning	fiṣ ṣabāḥ al bākir **في الصباح الباكر**
this morning	ṣabāḥ al yawm **صباح اليوم**
tomorrow morning	ṣabāḥ al ɣad **صباح الغد**
in the middle of the day	fi muntaṣif an nahār **في منتصف النهار**
in the afternoon	ba'd aẓ ẓuhr **بعد الظهر**
in the evening	fil masā' **في المساء**
tonight	masā' al yawm **مساء اليوم**
at night	bil layl **بالليل**
yesterday	ams **أمس**
today	al yawm **اليوم**
tomorrow	ɣadan **غداً**
the day after tomorrow	ba'd ɣad **بعد غد**
What day is it today?	fi ayy yawm naḥnu? **في أي يوم نحن؟**
It's ...	naḥnu fi ... **نحن في ...**
Monday	al iθnayn **الإثنين**
Tuesday	aθ θulāθā' **الثلاثاء**
Wednesday	al 'arbi'ā' **الأربعاء**
Thursday	al χamīs **الخميس**
Friday	al ʒum'a **الجمعة**
Saturday	as sabt **السبت**
Sunday	al aḥad **الأحد**

Greetings. Introductions

Hello.	as salāmu 'alaykum السلام عليكم
Pleased to meet you.	ana sa'īd ʒiddan bi liqā'ik أنا سعيد جدا بلقائك
Me too.	ana as'ad أنا أسعد
I'd like you to meet ...	awudd an u'arrifak bi ... أود أن أعرفك بـ ...
Nice to meet you.	furṣa sa'īda فرصة سعيدة

How are you?	kayf ḥālak? كيف حالك؟
My name is ...	ismi ... أسمي ...
His name is ...	ismuhu ... إسمه ...
Her name is ...	ismuha ... إسمها ...
What's your name?	ma smuka? ما اسمك؟
What's his name?	ma smuhu? ما اسمه؟
What's her name?	ma smuha? ما اسمها؟

What's your last name?	ma huwa ism 'ā'ilatak? ما هو إسم عائلتك؟
You can call me ...	yumkinak an tunādīni bi... يمكنك أن تناديني بـ...
Where are you from?	min ayna anta? من أين أنت؟
I'm from ...	ana min ... أنا من ...
What do you do for a living?	māða ta'mal? ماذا تعمل؟
Who is this?	man haða من هذا؟
Who is he?	man huwa? من هو؟
Who is she?	man hiya? من هي؟
Who are they?	man hum? من هم؟

This is ...	haða huwa /haðihi hiya/ ... هذا هو /هذه هي... /
my friend (masc.)	ṣadīqi صديقي
my friend (fem.)	ṣadīqati صديقتي
my husband	zawʒi زوجي
my wife	zawʒati زوجتي
my father	abi أبي
my mother	ummi أمي
my brother	aχi أخي
my son	ibni إبني
my daughter	ibnati إبنتي
This is our son.	haða huwa ibnuna هذا هو ابننا
This is our daughter.	haðihi hiya ibnatuna هذه هي ابنتنا
These are my children.	ha'ulā' awlādi هؤلاء أولادي
These are our children.	ha'ulā' awlāduna هؤلاء أولادنا

Farewells

Good bye!	as salāmu 'alaykum السلام عليكم
Bye! (inform.)	ma' as salāma مع السلامة
See you tomorrow.	ilal liqā' ɣadan إلى اللقاء غدا
See you soon.	ilal liqā' إلى اللقاء
See you at seven.	ilal liqā' as sā'a as sābi'a إلى اللقاء الساعة السابعة
Have fun!	atamanna laka waqtan ṭayyiban! أتمنى لكم وقتا طيبا!
Talk to you later.	ukallimuka lāḥiqan أكلمك لاحقا
Have a nice weekend.	'uṭlat usbū' sa'īda عطلة أسبوع سعيدة
Good night.	taṣbaḥ 'ala χayr تصبح على خير
It's time for me to go.	innahu waqt ðahābi إنه وقت ذهابي
I have to go.	yaʒib 'alayya an aðhab يجب علي أن أذهب
I will be right back.	sa'a'ūd ḥālan سأعود حالا
It's late.	al waqt muta'aχχar الوقت متأخر
I have to get up early.	yaʒib 'alayya an anhaḍ bākiran يجب علي أن أنهض باكرا
I'm leaving tomorrow.	innani uɣādir ɣadan إنني أغادر غدا
We're leaving tomorrow.	innana nuɣādir ɣadan إننا نغادر غدا
Have a nice trip!	riḥla sa'īda! رحلة سعيدة!
It was nice meeting you.	furṣa sa'īda فرصة سعيدة
It was nice talking to you.	kān laṭīf at taḥadduθ ma'ak كان لطيفا التحدث معك
Thanks for everything.	ʃukran 'ala kull ʃay' شكرا على كل شيء

I had a very good time.	qaḍayt waqt ʒayyidan **قضيت وقتا جيدا**
We had a very good time.	qaḍayna waqt ʒayyidan **قضينا وقتا جيدا**
It was really great.	kull ʃay' kān rā'i' **كل شيء كان رائعا**
I'm going to miss you.	sa'aʃtāq ilayk **سأشتاق إليك**
We're going to miss you.	sanaʃtāq ilayk **سنشتاق إليك**

Good luck!	bit tawfīq! ma' as salāma! **!مع السلامة !بالتوفيق**
Say hi to ...	taḥīyyāti li ... **تحياتي لـ...**

Foreign language

I don't understand.	ana la afham أنا لا أفهم
Write it down, please.	uktubha min faḍlak إكتبها من فضلك
Do you speak ...?	hal tatakallam bi ...? هل تتكلم بـ...؟
I speak a little bit of ...	atakallam bi ... qalīlan أتكلم بـ ... قليلا
English	al inʒlīziyya الإنجليزية
Turkish	at turkiyya التركية
Arabic	al ʿarabiyya العربية
French	al faransiyya الفرنسية
German	al almāniyya الألمانية
Italian	al iṭāliyya الإيطالية
Spanish	al isbāniyya الإسبانية
Portuguese	al burtuɣāliyya البرتغالية
Chinese	aṣ ṣīniyya الصينية
Japanese	al yabāniyya اليابانية
Can you repeat that, please.	hal yumkinuka tikrār min faḍlak? هل يمكنك تكرار من فضلك؟
I understand.	ana afham انا أفهم
I don't understand.	ana la afham أنا لا أفهم
Please speak more slowly.	takallam bi buṭʾ akθar min faḍlak تكلم ببطء أكثر من فضلك
Is that correct? (Am I saying it right?)	hal haða ṣaḥīḥ? هل هذا صحيح؟
What is this? (What does this mean?)	māða yaʿni? ماذا يعني؟

Apologies

Excuse me, please.	la tu'āχiðni min faḍlak لا تؤاخذني من فضلك
I'm sorry.	ana 'āṣif أنا آسف
I'm really sorry.	ana 'āsif ʒiddan أنا آسف جدا
Sorry, it's my fault.	ana 'āsif innaha ɣalṭati أنا آسف، إنها غلطتي
My mistake.	χaṭa'i خطئي
May I ...?	hal yumkinuni ...? هل يمكنني ...؟
Do you mind if I ...?	hal tumāni' law ...? هل تمانع لو ...؟
It's OK.	laysa hunāk ayy muʃkila ليس هناك أي مشكلة
It's all right.	kull ʃay' 'ala ma yurām كل شيء على ما يرام
Don't worry about it.	la taqlaq لا تقلق

Agreement

Yes.	na'am نعم
Yes, sure.	aʒl أجل
OK (Good!)	ḥasanan حسنا
Very well.	ʒayyid ʒiddan جيد جدا
Certainly!	bit ta'kīd! !بالتأكيد
I agree.	ana muwāfiq أنا موافق
That's correct.	haða ṣaḥīḥ هذا صحيح
That's right.	haða ṣaḥīḥ هذا صحيح
You're right.	kalāmak ṣaḥīḥ كلامك صحيح
I don't mind.	ana la umāni' أنا لا أمانع
Absolutely right.	anta muhiqq tamāman أنت محق تماما
It's possible.	innahu min al mumkin إنه من الممكن
That's a good idea.	innaha fikra ʒayyida إنها فكرة جيدة
I can't say no.	la astaṭī' an aqūl la لا أستطيع أن أقول لا
I'd be happy to.	sa'akūn sa'īdan سأكون سعيدا
With pleasure.	bi kull surūr بكل سرور

Refusal. Expressing doubt

No.	la لا
Certainly not.	ṭab'an la طبعا لا
I don't agree.	lastu muwāfiq لست موافقا
I don't think so.	la aẓunn ðalika لا أظن ذلك
It's not true.	laysa haða ṣaḥīḥ ليس هذا صحيحا
You are wrong.	axṭa'ta أخطأت
I think you are wrong.	aẓunn annaka axṭa't أظن أنك أخطأت
I'm not sure.	lastu muta'akkid لست متأكدا
It's impossible.	haða mustaḥīl هذا مستحيل
Nothing of the kind (sort)!	la ʃay' min haðan naw' لا شيء من هذا النوع
The exact opposite.	al 'aks tamāman العكس تماما
I'm against it.	ana ḍidda ðalika أنا ضد ذلك
I don't care.	la yuhimmuni ðalika لا يهمني ذلك
I have no idea.	laysa ladayya ayy fikra ليس لدي أي فكرة
I doubt it.	aʃukk fe ðalik أشك في ذلك
Sorry, I can't.	'āsif la astaṭī' آسف، لا أستطيع
Sorry, I don't want to.	'āsif la urīd ðalika آسف، لا أريد ذلك
Thank you, but I don't need this.	ʃukran, wa lakinnani la aḥtāʒ ila ðalika شكرا، ولكنني لا أحتاج إلى ذلك
It's getting late.	al waqt muta'axxar الوقت متأخر

I have to get up early.	yaʒib 'alayya an anhaḍ bākiran **يجب علي أن أنهض باكرا**
I don't feel well.	la aʃur bi χayr **لا أشعر بخير**

Expressing gratitude

Thank you.	ʃukran **شكرا**
Thank you very much.	ʃukran ʒazīlan **شكرا جزيلا**
I really appreciate it.	ana uqaddir ðalika ḥaqqan **أنا أقدر ذلك حقا**
I'm really grateful to you.	ana mumtann lak ʒiddan **أنا ممتن لك جدا**
We are really grateful to you.	naḥnu mumtannīn lak ʒiddan **نحن ممتنون لك جدا**
Thank you for your time.	ʃukran ʿala waqtak **شكرا على وقتك**
Thanks for everything.	ʃukran ʿala kull ʃayʾ **شكرا على كل شيء**
Thank you for ...	ʃukran ʿala ... **شكرا على ...**
your help	musāʿadatak **مساعدتك**
a nice time	al waqt al laṭīf **الوقت اللطيف**
a wonderful meal	waʒba rāʾiʿa **وجبة رائعة**
a pleasant evening	amsiyya mumtiʿa **أمسية ممتعة**
a wonderful day	yawm rāʾiʿ **يوم رائع**
an amazing journey	riḥla mudhiʃa **رحلة مدهشة**
Don't mention it.	la ʃukr ʿala wāʒib **لا شكر على واجب**
You are welcome.	al ʿafw **العفو**
Any time.	fi ayy waqt **في أي وقت**
My pleasure.	bi kull surūr **بكل سرور**
Forget it.	insa al amr **إنس الأمر**
Don't worry about it.	la taqlaq **لا تقلق**

Congratulations. Best wishes

Congratulations!	uhanni'uka! أهنئك!
Happy birthday!	ʿīd milād saʿīd! عيد ميلاد سعيد!
Merry Christmas!	ʿīd milād saʿīd! عيد ميلاد سعيد!
Happy New Year!	sana ʒadīda saʿīda! سنة جديدة سعيدة!
Happy Easter!	ʿīd fiṣḥ saʿīd! عيد فصح سعيد!
Happy Hanukkah!	hanūka saʿīda! هانوكا سعيدة!
I'd like to propose a toast.	awudd an aqtariḥ naχb أود أن أقترح نخبا
Cheers!	fi siḥḥatak في صحتك
Let's drink to ...!	daʿawna naʃrab fi ...! دعونا نشرب في ...!
To our success!	naʒāḥna نجاحنا
To your success!	naʒaḥak نجاحك
Good luck!	bit tawfīq! بالتوفيق!
Have a nice day!	atamanna laka nahāran saʿīdan! أتمنى لك نهارا سعيدا!
Have a good holiday!	atamanna laka ʿuṭla ṭayyiba! أتمنى لك عطلة طيبة!
Have a safe journey!	atamanna laka riḥla āmina! أتمنى لك رحلة آمنة!
I hope you get better soon!	atamanna bi annaka satataḥassan qarīban أتمنى بأنك ستتحسن قريبا

Socializing

Why are you sad?	limāða anta ḥazīn? **لماذا أنت حزين؟**
Smile! Cheer up!	ibtasim! **إبتسم!**
Are you free tonight?	hal anta ḥurr haðihil layla? **هل أنت حر هذه الليلة؟**
May I offer you a drink?	hal tawudd an taʃrab ʃay'? **هل تود أن تشرب شيئا؟**
Would you like to dance?	hal tawudd an tarquṣ? **هل تود أن ترقص؟**
Let's go to the movies.	da'awna naðhab ilas sinima **دعونا نذهب إلى السينما**
May I invite you to ...?	hal yumkinuni an ad'ūk ila ...? **هل يمكنني أن أدعوك إلى ...؟**
a restaurant	maṭ'am **مطعم**
the movies	as sinima **السينما**
the theater	al masraḥ **المسرح**
go for a walk	tamʃiya **تمشية**
At what time?	fi ayy sā'a? **في أي ساعة؟**
tonight	haðal masā' **هذا المساء**
at six	as sā'a as sādisa **الساعة السادسة**
at seven	as sā'a as sābi'a **الساعة السابعة**
at eight	as sā'a aθ θāmina **الساعة الثامنة**
at nine	as sā'a at tāsi'a **الساعة التاسعة**
Do you like it here?	hal yu'ʒibak al makān? **هل يعجبك المكان؟**
Are you here with someone?	hal anta huna ma' aḥad? **هل أنت هنا مع أحد؟**
I'm with my friend.	ana ma' ṣadīq **أنا مع صديق**

I'm with my friends.	ana ma' aṣdiqā' أنا مع أصدقاء
No, I'm alone.	la, ana li waḥdi لا، أنا لوحدي
Do you have a boyfriend?	hal 'indak ṣadīq? هل عندك صديق؟
I have a boyfriend.	ana 'indi ṣadīq أنا عندي صديق
Do you have a girlfriend?	hal 'indak ṣadīqa? هل عندك صديقة؟
I have a girlfriend.	ana 'indi ṣadīqa أنا عندي صديقة
Can I see you again?	hal yumkinuni ru'yatak marra uχra? هل يمكنني رؤيتك مرة أخرى؟
Can I call you?	hal astaṭī' an attaṣil bik? هل أستطيع أن أتصل بك؟
Call me. (Give me a call.)	ittaṣil bi إتصل بي
What's your number?	ma raqmak? ما رقمك؟
I miss you.	aʃtāq ilayk أشتاق إليك
You have a beautiful name.	ismak ʒamīl إسمك جميل
I love you.	uḥibbak أحبك
Will you marry me?	hal tatazawwaʒīnani? هل تتزوجيللي؟
You're kidding!	anta tamzaḥ! أنت تمزح!
I'm just kidding.	ana amzaḥ faqaṭ أنا أمزح فقط
Are you serious?	hal anta gadd? هل أنت جاد؟
I'm serious.	ana gādd أنا جاد
Really?!	ṣaḥīḥ? صحيح؟
It's unbelievable!	haða ɣayr ma'qūl! هذا غير معقول!
I don't believe you.	la uṣaddiqak لا أصدقك
I can't.	ana la astaṭī' أنا لا أستطيع
I don't know.	la a'rif أنا لا أعرف
I don't understand you.	la afhamak أنا لا أفهمك

Please go away.	min faḍlak iðhab min huna **من فضلك إذهب من هنا**
Leave me alone!	utrukni li waḥdi! **أتركني لوحدي!**

I can't stand him.	ana la uṭīquhu **أنا لا أطيقه**
You are disgusting!	anta muqrif **أنت مقرف**
I'll call the police!	hattlob el ʃorṭa **سأتصل بالشرطة**

Sharing impressions. Emotions

I like it.	yu'ʒibuni ðalika **يعجبني ذلك**
Very nice.	ʒamīl ʒiddan **جميل جدا**
That's great!	haða rā'i' **هذا رائع**
It's not bad.	la ba's bihi **لا بأس به**

I don't like it.	la yu'ʒibuni ðalika **لا يعجبني ذلك**
It's not good.	laysa ʒayyid **ليس جيدا**
It's bad.	haða sayyi' **هذا سيء**
It's very bad.	haða sayyi' ʒiddan **هذا سيء جدا**
It's disgusting.	haða muqrif **هذا مقرف**

I'm happy.	ana sa'īd /sa'īda/ **أنا سعيد /سعيدة/**
I'm content	ana mabsūṭ /mabsūṭa/ **أنا مبسوط /مبسوطة/**
I'm in love.	ana uḥibb **أنا أحب**
I'm calm.	ana hādi' /hādi'a/ **أنا هادئ /هادئة/**
I'm bored.	aʃur bil malal **أشعر بالملل**

I'm tired.	ana ta'bān /ta'bāna/ **أنا تعبان /تعبانة/**
I'm sad.	ana ḥazīn /ḥazīna/ **أنا حزين /حزينة/**
I'm frightened.	ana χā'if /χā'ifa/ **أنا خائف /خائفة/**
I'm angry.	ana ɣāḍib /ɣāḍiba/ **أنا غاضب /غاضبة/**
I'm worried.	ana qaliq /qaliqa/ **أنا قلق /قلقة/**

I'm nervous.	ana mutawattir /mutawattira/ **أنا متوتر /متوترة/**

I'm jealous. (envious)	ana ɣayūr /ɣayūra/ **أنا غيور /غيورة/**
I'm surprised.	ana mutafāʒiʾ /mutafāʒiʾa/ **أنا متفاجئ /متفاجئة/**
I'm perplexed.	ana ḥāʾir /ḥāʾira/ **أنا حائر /حائرة/**

Problems. Accidents

I've got a problem.	ʿindi muʃkila **عندي مشكلة**
We've got a problem.	ʿindana muʃkila **عندنا مشكلة**
I'm lost.	aḍaʿt ṭarīqi **أضعت طريقي**
I missed the last bus (train).	fātatni ʾāχir ḥāfila **فاتتني آخر حافلة**
I don't have any money left.	laysa ladayya ayy māl **ليس لدي أي مال**
I've lost my ...	faqadt ... **فقدت ...**
Someone stole my ...	saraqu minni ... **سرقوا مني ...**
passport	ʒawāz as safar **جواز السفر**
wallet	al maḥfaẓa **المحفظة**
papers	al awrāq **الأوراق**
ticket	at taðkira **التذكرة**
money	an nuqūd **النقود**
handbag	aʃ ʃanṭa **الشنطة**
camera	al kamira **الكاميرا**
laptop	al kumbyūtir al maḥmūl **الكمبيوتر المحمول**
tablet computer	al kumbyūtir al lawḥiy **الكمبيوتر اللوحى**
mobile phone	at tilifūn al maḥmūl **التليفون المحمول**
Help me!	sāʿidni! **ساعدني!**
What's happened?	māða ḥadaθ? **ماذا حدث؟**
fire	ḥarīqa **حريقة**

shooting	iṭlāq an nār **إطلاق النار**
murder	qatl **قتل**
explosion	infiʒār **إنفجار**
fight	χināqa **خناقة**

Call the police!	ittaṣil biʃ ʃurṭa! **إتصل بالشرطة!**
Please hurry up!	bi sur'a min faḍlak! **بسرعة من فضلك!**
I'm looking for the police station.	abḥaθ 'an qism aʃ ʃurṭa **أبحث عن قسم الشرطة**
I need to make a call.	urīd iʒrā' mukālama hātifiyya **أريد إجراء مكالمة هاتفية**
May I use your phone?	hal yumkinuni an astaχdim tilifūnak? **هل يمكنني أن أستخدم تليفونك؟**

I've been …	laqat ta'arraḍt li … **لقد تعرضت لـ...**
mugged	sirqa **سرقة**
robbed	sirqa **سرقة**
raped	iɣtiṣāb **إغتصاب**
attacked (beaten up)	i'tidā' **إعتداء**

Are you all right?	hal anta bi χayr? **هل أنت بخير؟**
Did you see who it was?	hal ra'ayt man kān ðalik? **هل رأيت من كان ذلك؟**
Would you be able to recognize the person?	hal tastaṭī' at ta'arruf 'alayhi? **هل ستستطيع التعرف عليه؟**
Are you sure?	hal anta muta'kked? **هل أنت متأكد؟**

Please calm down.	ihda' min faḍlak **إهدأ من فضلك**
Take it easy!	hawwin 'alayk! **هون عليك!**
Don't worry!	la taqlaq! **لا تقلق!**
Everything will be fine.	kull ʃay' sayakūn 'ala ma yurām **كل شيء سيكون على ما يرام**
Everything's all right.	kull ʃay' 'ala ma yurām **كل شيء على ما يرام**
Come here, please.	ta'āla huna law samaḥt **تعال هنا لو سمحت**

I have some questions for you.	ʿindi lak asʾila **عندي لك أسئلة**
Wait a moment, please.	intaẓir laḥẓa min faḍlak **إنتظر لحظة من فضلك**
Do you have any I.D.?	hal ʿindak biṭāqa ʃaχsiyya? **هل عندك بطاقة شخصية؟**
Thanks. You can leave now.	ʃukran. yumkinuka al muɣādara al ʾān **شكرا. يمكنك المغادرة الآن**
Hands behind your head!	ḍaʿ yadayk χalfa raʾsak! **ضع يديك خلف رأسك!**
You're under arrest!	anta mawqūf! **أنت موقوف!**

Health problems

Please help me.	sā'idni min faḍlak **ساعدني من فضلك**
I don't feel well.	la aʃur bi χayr **لا أشعر بخير**
My husband doesn't feel well.	zawʒi la yaʃur bi χayr **زوجي لا يشعر بخير**
My son ...	ibni ... **إبني ...**
My father ...	abi ... **أبي ...**
My wife doesn't feel well.	zawʒati la taʃur bi χayr **زوجتي لا تشعر بخير**
My daughter ...	ibnati ... **إبنتي ...**
My mother ...	ummi ... **أمي ...**
I've got a ...	ana 'indi ... **أنا عندي ...**
headache	ṣudā' **صداع**
sore throat	iltihāb fil ḥalq **إلتهاب في الحلق**
stomach ache	maɣaṣ **مغص**
toothache	alam asnān **ألم أسنان**
I feel dizzy.	aʃur bid dawār **أشعر بالدوار**
He has a fever.	'indahu ḥumma **عنده حمى**
She has a fever.	'indaha ḥumma **عندها حمى**
I can't breathe.	la astaṭī' at tanaffus **لا أستطيع التنفس**
I'm short of breath.	aʃur bi ḍīq at tanaffus **أشعر بضيق التنفس**
I am asthmatic.	u'āni min ar rabw **أعاني من الربو**
I am diabetic.	ana 'indi maraḍ as sukkar **أنا عندي مرض السكر**

I can't sleep.	la astaṭīʿ an anām لا أستطيع أن أنام
food poisoning	tasammum ɣiðā'iy تسمم غذائي
It hurts here.	aʃur bi alam huna أشعر بألم هنا
Help me!	sā'idni! ساعدني!
I am here!	ana huna! أنا هنا!
We are here!	naḥnu huna! نحن هنا!
Get me out of here!	aɣraʒūni min huna أخرجوني من هنا!
I need a doctor.	ana aḥtāʒ ila ṭabīb أنا أحتاج إلى طبيب
I can't move.	la astaṭīʿ an ataḥarrak لا أستطيع أن أتحرك
I can't move my legs.	la astaṭīʿ an uḥarrik riʒlayya لا أستطيع أن أحرك رجلي
I have a wound.	'indi ʒurḥ عندي جرح
Is it serious?	hal al amr ɣaṭīr? هل الأمر خطير؟
My documents are in my pocket.	awrāqi fi ʒaybi أوراقي في جيبي
Calm down!	ihda'! إهدأ!
May I use your phone?	hal yumkinuni an astaɣdim tilifūnak? هل يمكنني أن أستخدم تليفونك؟
Call an ambulance!	ittaṣil bil is'āf! إتصل بالإسعاف!
It's urgent!	al amr 'āʒil! الأمر عاجل!
It's an emergency!	innaha ḥāla ṭāri'a! إنها حالة طارئة!
Please hurry up!	bi sur'a min faḍlak! بسرعة من فضلك!
Would you please call a doctor?	ittaṣil biṭ ṭabib min faḍlak? إتصل بالطبيب من فضلك
Where is the hospital?	ayna al mustaʃfa? أين المستشفى؟
How are you feeling?	kayf taʃur al 'ān كيف تشعر الآن؟
Are you all right?	hal anta bi ɣayr? هل أنت بخير؟
What's happened?	māða ḥadaθ? ماذا حدث؟

I feel better now.	aʃʿur bi taḥassun al ʾān **أشعر بتحسن الآن**
It's OK.	la baʾs **لا بأس**
It's all right.	kull ʃayʾ ʿala ma yurām **كل شيء على ما يرام**

At the pharmacy

pharmacy (drugstore)	ṣaydaliyya **صيدلية**
24-hour pharmacy	ṣaydaliyya arba' wa 'iʃrīn sā'a **صيدلية 24 ساعة**
Where is the closest pharmacy?	ayna aqrab ṣaydaliyya? **أين أقرب صيدلية؟**
Is it open now?	hal hiya maftūḥa al 'ān? **هل هي مفتوحة الآن؟**
At what time does it open?	mata taftaḥ? **متى تفتح؟**
At what time does it close?	mata tuɣliq? **متى تغلق؟**
Is it far?	hal hiya ba'īda? **هل هي بعيدة؟**
Can I get there on foot?	hal yumkinuni an aṣil ila hunāk māʃiyan? **هل يمكنني أن أصل إلى هناك ماشيا؟**
Can you show me on the map?	arīni 'alal χarīṭa min faḍlak **أريني على الخريطة من فضلك**
Please give me something for ...	min faḍlak a'ṭini ʃay' li ... **من فضلك أعطني شيئا لـ ...**
a headache	aṣ ṣudā' **الصداع**
a cough	as su'āl **السعال**
a cold	al bard **البرد**
the flu	al influenza **الأنفلوانزا**
a fever	al ḥumma **الحمى**
a stomach ache	el maɣaṣ **المغص**
nausea	a ɣaθayān **الغثيان**
diarrhea	al ishāl **الإسهال**
constipation	al imsāk **الإمساك**
pain in the back	alam fiẓ ẓahr **ألم في الظهر**

chest pain	alam fiṣ ṣadr ألم في الصدر
side stitch	ɣurza ʒānibiyya غرزة جانبية
abdominal pain	alam fil baṭn ألم في البطن

pill	ḥabba حبة
ointment, cream	marham, krīm مرهم، كريم
syrup	ʃarāb شراب
spray	baχχāχ بخاخ
drops	qaṭarāt قطرات

You need to go to the hospital.	'alayk an taðhab ilal mustaʃfa عليك أن تذهب إلى المستشفى
health insurance	ta'mīn ṣiḥḥiy تأمين صحي
prescription	waṣfa ṭibbiyya وصفة طبية
insect repellant	ṭārid lil ḥaʃarāt طارد للحشرات
Band Aid	laṣqa lil ʒurūḥ لصقة للجروح

The bare minimum

Excuse me, ...	law samaḥt, ... **لو سمحت، ...**
Hello.	as salāmu 'alaykum **السلام عليكم**
Thank you.	ʃukran **شكرا**
Good bye.	ma' as salāma **مع السلامة**
Yes.	na'am **نعم**
No.	la **لا**
I don't know.	la a'rif **لا أعرف**
Where? | Where to? | When?	ayna? | ila ayna? | mata? **أين؟ | إلى أين؟ | متى؟**
I need ...	ana aḥtāʒ ila ... **أنا أحتاج إلى...**
I want ...	ana urīd ... **أنا أريد ...**
Do you have ...?	hal 'indak ...? **هل عندك...؟**
Is there a ... here?	hal yūʒad huna ...? **هل يوجد هنا ...؟**
May I ...?	hal yumkinuni ...? **هل يمكنني...؟**
..., please (polite request)	... min faḍlak **من فضلك ...**
I'm looking for ...	abḥaθ 'an ... **أبحث عن ...**
restroom	ḥammām **حمام**
ATM	mākīnat ṣarrāf 'āliy **ماكينة صراف آلي**
pharmacy (drugstore)	ṣaydaliyya **صيدلية**
hospital	mustaʃfa **مستشفى**
police station	qism aʃ ʃurṭa **قسم شرطة**
subway	mitru al anfāq **مترو الأنفاق**

taxi	taksi **تاكسي**
train station	maḥaṭṭat al qiṭār **محطة القطار**

My name is ...	ismi ... **إسمي...**
What's your name?	ma smuka? **ما اسمك؟**
Could you please help me?	sāʿidni min faḍlak **ساعدني من فضلك**
I've got a problem.	ʿindi muʃkila **عندي مشكلة**
I don't feel well.	la aʃʿur bi χayr **لا أشعر بخير**
Call an ambulance!	ittaṣil bil isʿāf! **إتصل بالإسعاف!**
May I make a call?	hal yumkinuni iʒrāʾ mukālama tilifūniyya? **هل يمكنني إجراء مكالمة هاتفية؟**

I'm sorry.	ana ʾāṣif **أنا آسف**
You're welcome.	al ʿafw **العفو**

I, me	ana **أنا**
you (inform.)	anta **أنت**
he	huwa **هو**
she	hiya **هي**
they (masc.)	hum **هم**
they (fem.)	hum **هم**
we	naḥnu **نحن**
you (pl)	antum **أنتم**
you (sg, form.)	ḥaḍritak **حضرتك**

ENTRANCE	duχūl **دخول**
EXIT	χurūʒ **خروج**
OUT OF ORDER	muʿaṭṭal **معطل**
CLOSED	muɣlaq **مغلق**

OPEN	maftūḥ **مفتوح**
FOR WOMEN	lis sayyidāt **للسيدات**
FOR MEN	lir riʒāl **للرجال**

CONCISE DICTIONARY

This section contains more than 1,500 useful words arranged alphabetically. The dictionary includes a lot of gastronomic terms and will be helpful when ordering food at a restaurant or buying groceries

T&P Books Publishing

DICTIONARY CONTENTS

1. Time. Calendar

time	wa't (m)	وقت
hour	sā'a (f)	ساعة
half an hour	noṣṣ sā'a (m)	نصّ ساعة
minute	de'ī'a (f)	دقيقة
second	sanya (f)	ثانية
today (adv)	el naharda	النهارده
tomorrow (adv)	bokra	بكرة
yesterday (adv)	embāreḥ	امبارح
Monday	el etneyn (m)	الإتنين
Tuesday	el talāt (m)	التلات
Wednesday	el arbe'ā' (m)	الأربعاء
Thursday	el χamīs (m)	الخميس
Friday	el gom'a (m)	الجمعة
Saturday	el sabt (m)	السبت
Sunday	el aḥad (m)	الأحد
day	yome (m)	يوم
working day	yome 'amal (m)	يوم عمل
public holiday	agāza rasmiya (f)	أجازة رسميّة
weekend	nehāyet el osbū' (f)	نهاية الأسبوع
week	osbū' (m)	أسبوع
last week (adv)	el esbū' elly fāt	الأسبوع اللي فات
next week (adv)	el esbū' elly gayī	الأسبوع اللي جاي
sunrise	ʃorū' el ʃams (m)	شروق الشمس
sunset	ɣorūb el ʃams (m)	غروب الشمس
in the morning	fel ṣobḥ	في الصبح
in the afternoon	ba'd el ḍohr	بعد الظهر
in the evening	bel leyl	بالليل
tonight (this evening)	el naharda bel leyl	النهاردة بالليل
at night	bel leyl	بالليل
midnight	noṣṣ el leyl (m)	نصّ الليل
January	yanāyer (m)	يناير
February	febrāyer (m)	فبراير
March	māres (m)	مارس
April	ebrīl (m)	إبريل
May	māyo (m)	مايو
June	yonyo (m)	يونيو

July	yolyo (m)	يوليو
August	oɣosṭos (m)	أغسطس
September	sebtamber (m)	سبتمبر
October	oktober (m)	أكتوبر
November	november (m)	نوفمبر
December	desember (m)	ديسمبر
in spring	fel rabee'	في الربيع
in summer	fel ṣeyf	في الصيف
in fall	fel χarīf	في الخريف
in winter	fel ʃetā'	في الشتاء
month	ʃahr (m)	شهر
season (summer, etc.)	faṣl (m)	فصل
year	sana (f)	سنة
century	qarn (m)	قرن

2. Numbers. Numerals

digit, figure	raqam (m)	رقم
number	'adad (m)	عدد
minus sign	nā'eṣ (m)	ناقص
plus sign	zā'ed (m)	زائد
sum, total	magmū' (m)	مجموع
first (adj)	awwel	أوّل
second (adj)	tāny	ثاني
third (adj)	tālet	ثالث
0 zero	ṣefr	صفر
1 one	wāḥed	واحد
2 two	etneyn	إتنين
3 three	talāta	ثلاثة
4 four	arba'a	أربعة
5 five	χamsa	خمسة
6 six	setta	ستّة
7 seven	sab'a	سبعة
8 eight	tamanya	ثمانية
9 nine	tes'a	تسعة
10 ten	'aʃara	عشرة
11 eleven	ḥedāʃar	حداشر
12 twelve	etnāʃar	إتناشر
13 thirteen	talattāʃar	تلاتّاشر
14 fourteen	arba'tāʃer	أربعتاشر
15 fifteen	χamastāʃer	خمستاشر
16 sixteen	settāʃar	ستّاشر
17 seventeen	saba'tāʃar	سبعتاشر

18 eighteen	tamantāʃar	تمنتاشر
19 nineteen	tesʿatāʃar	تسعتاشر
20 twenty	ʿeʃrīn	عشرين
30 thirty	talatīn	ثلاثين
40 forty	arbeʿīn	أربعين
50 fifty	χamsīn	خمسين
60 sixty	settīn	ستّين
70 seventy	sabʿīn	سبعين
80 eighty	tamanīn	ثمانين
90 ninety	tesʿīn	تسعين
100 one hundred	miya	ميّة
200 two hundred	meteyn	ميتين
300 three hundred	toltomiya	تلتميّة
400 four hundred	robʿomiya	ربعميّة
500 five hundred	χomsomiya	خمسميّة
600 six hundred	sotomiya	ستميّة
700 seven hundred	sobʿomiya	سبعميّة
800 eight hundred	tomnome'a	ثمنمئة
900 nine hundred	tosʿomiya	تسعميّة
1000 one thousand	alf	ألف
10000 ten thousand	ʿaʃaret ʾālāf	عشرة آلاف
one hundred thousand	mīt alf	ميت ألف
million	millyon (m)	مليون
billion	millyār (m)	مليار

3. Humans. Family

man (adult male)	rāgel (m)	راجل
young man	ʃāb (m)	شاب
teenager	morāheq (m)	مراهق
woman	set (f)	ست
girl (young woman)	bent (f)	بنت
age	ʿomr (m)	عمر
adult (adj)	rāʃed (m)	راشد
middle-aged (adj)	fe montaṣaf el ʿomr	في منتصف العمر
elderly (adj)	ʿagūz	عجوز
old (adj)	ʿagūz	عجوز
old man	ʿagūz (m)	عجوز
old woman	ʿagūza (f)	عجوزة
retirement	maʿāʃ (m)	معاش
to retire (from job)	oḥīl ʿala el maʿāʃ	أحيل على المعاش
retiree	motaqāʿed (m)	متقاعد

mother	walda (f)	والدة
father	wāled (m)	والد
son	walad (m)	ولد
daughter	bent (f)	بنت
brother	aχ (m)	أخ
elder brother	el aχ el kibīr (m)	الأخ الكبير
younger brother	el aχ el ṣoɣeyyir (m)	الأخ الصغير
sister	oχt (f)	أخت
elder sister	el uχt el kibīra (f)	الأخت الكبيرة
younger sister	el uχt el ṣoɣeyyira (f)	الأخت الصغيرة
parents	waldeyn (du)	والدين
child	ṭefl (m)	طفل
children	aṭfāl (pl)	أطفال
stepmother	merāt el abb (f)	مرات الأب
stepfather	goze el omm (m)	جوز الأم
grandmother	gedda (f)	جدّة
grandfather	gadd (m)	جدّ
grandson	ḥafīd (m)	حفيد
granddaughter	ḥafīda (f)	حفيدة
grandchildren	aḥfād (pl)	أحفاد
uncle	ʿamm (m), χāl (m)	عمّ, خال
aunt	ʿamma (f), χāla (f)	عمة, خالة
nephew	ibn el aχ (m), ibn el uχt (m)	إبن الأخ, إبن الأخت
niece	bint el aχ (f), bint el uχt (f)	بنت الأخ, بنت الأخت
wife	goza (f)	جوزة
husband	goze (m)	جوز
married (masc.)	metgawwez	متجوّز
married (fem.)	metgawweza	متجوّزة
widow	armala (f)	أرملة
widower	armal (m)	أرمل
name (first name)	esm (m)	اسم
surname (last name)	esm el ʿaʾela (m)	اسم العائلة
relative	ʾarīb (m)	قريب
friend (masc.)	ṣadīq (m)	صديق
friendship	ṣadāqa (f)	صداقة
partner	rafīʾ (m)	رفيق
superior (n)	el arfaʿ maqāman (m)	الأرفع مقاماً
colleague	zamīl (m)	زميل
neighbors	gerān (pl)	جيران

4. Human body

organism (body)	ʿoḍw (m)	عضو
body	gesm (m)	جسم

heart	ʾalb (m)	قلب
blood	damm (m)	دم
brain	mokχ (m)	مخ
nerve	ʿaṣab (m)	عصب
bone	ʿaḍm (m)	عظم
skeleton	haykal ʿazmy (m)	هيكل عظمي
spine (backbone)	ʿamūd faqry (m)	عمود فقري
rib	ḍelʿ (m)	ضلع
skull	gomgoma (f)	جمجمة
muscle	ʿaḍala (f)	عضلة
lungs	reʾateyn (du)	رئتين
skin	boʃra (m)	بشرة
head	raʾs (m)	رأس
face	weʃ (m)	وش
nose	manaχīr (m)	مناخير
forehead	gabha (f)	جبهة
cheek	χadd (m)	خدّ
mouth	boʾ (m)	بوء
tongue	lesān (m)	لسان
tooth	senna (f)	سنّة
lips	ʃafāyef (pl)	شفايف
chin	daʾʾn (m)	دقن
ear	wedn (f)	ودن
neck	raʾaba (f)	رقبة
throat	zore (m)	زور
eye	ʿeyn (f)	عين
pupil	ḥadʾa (f)	حدقة
eyebrow	ḥāgeb (m)	حاجب
eyelash	remʃ (m)	رمش
hair	ʃaʿr (m)	شعر
hairstyle	tasrīḥa (f)	تسريحة
mustache	ʃanab (pl)	شنب
beard	leḥya (f)	لحية
to have (a beard, etc.)	ʿando	عنده
bald (adj)	aṣlaʿ	أصلع
hand	yad (m)	يد
arm	derāʿ (f)	دراع
finger	ṣobāʿ (m)	صباع
nail	ḍefr (m)	ضفر
palm	kaff (f)	كفّ
shoulder	ketf (f)	كتف
leg	regl (f)	رجل
foot	qadam (f)	قدم

knee	rokba (f)	ركبة
heel	ka'b (m)	كعب
back	ḍahr (m)	ضهر
waist	wesṭ (f)	وسط
beauty mark	ʃāma (f)	شامة
birthmark (café au lait spot)	waḥma	وحمة

5. Medicine. Diseases. Drugs

health	ṣeḥḥa (f)	صحّة
well (not sick)	salīm	سليم
sickness	maraḍ (m)	مرض
to be sick	mereḍ	مرض
ill, sick (adj)	marīḍ	مريض
cold (illness)	zokām (m)	زكام
to catch a cold	gālo bard	جاله برد
tonsillitis	eltehāb el lawzateyn (m)	إلتهاب اللوزتين
pneumonia	eltehāb ra'awy (m)	إلتهاب رئوي
flu, influenza	influenza (f)	إنفلونزا
runny nose (coryza)	raʃ-ḥ fel anf (m)	رشح في الأنف
cough	koḥḥa (f)	كحّة
to cough (vi)	kaḥḥ	كحّ
to sneeze (vi)	'aṭas	عطس
stroke	sakta (f)	سكتة
heart attack	azma 'albiya (f)	أزمة قلبية
allergy	ḥasasiya (f)	حساسيّة
asthma	rabw (m)	ربو
diabetes	dā' el sokkary (m)	داء السكّري
tumor	waram (m)	ورم
cancer	saraṭān (m)	سرطان
alcoholism	edmān el χamr (m)	إدمان الخمر
AIDS	el eydz (m)	الايدز
fever	ḥomma (f)	حمّى
seasickness	dawār el baḥr (m)	دوار البحر
bruise (hématome)	kadma (f)	كدمة
bump (lump)	tawarrom (m)	تورّم
to limp (vi)	'arag	عرج
dislocation	χal' (m)	خلع
to dislocate (vt)	χala'	خلع
fracture	kasr (m)	كسر
burn (injury)	ḥar' (m)	حرق
injury	eṣāba (f)	إصابة

pain, ache	alam (m)	ألم
toothache	alam asnān (m)	ألم الأسنان
to sweat (perspire)	‘ere’	عرق
deaf (adj)	aṭraʃ	أطرش
mute (adj)	aχras	أخرس
immunity	manā‘a (f)	مناعة
virus	virūs (m)	فيروس
microbe	mikrūb (m)	ميكروب
bacterium	garsūma (f)	جرثومة
infection	‘adwa (f)	عدوى
hospital	mostaʃfa (m)	مستشفى
cure	ʃefā’ (m)	شفاء
to vaccinate (vt)	laqqaḥ	لقّح
to be in a coma	kān fi ḥālet ɣaybūba	كان في حالة غيبوبة
intensive care	el ‘enāya el morakkaza (f)	العناية المركّزة
symptom	‘araḍ (m)	عرض
pulse	nabḍ (m)	نبض

6. Feelings. Emotions. Conversation

I, me	ana	أنا
you (masc.)	enta	أنت
you (fem.)	enty	أنت
he	howwa	هوّ
she	hiya	هي
we	eḥna	إحنا
you (to a group)	antom	أنتم
they	hamm	هم
Hello! (form.)	assalamu ‘alaykum!	السلام عليكم!
Good morning!	ṣabāḥ el χeyr!	صباح الخير!
Good afternoon!	neharak saʿīd!	نهارك سعيد!
Good evening!	masā’ el χeyr!	مساء الخير!
to say hello	sallem	سلّم
to greet (vt)	sallem ‘ala	سلّم على
How are you?	ezzayek?	ازّيك؟
Bye-Bye! Goodbye!	ma‘ el salāma!	مع السلامة!
Thank you!	ʃokran!	شكراً!
feelings	maʃā‘er (pl)	مشاعر
to be hungry	‘āyez ’ākol	عايز آكل
to be thirsty	‘āyez aʃrab	عايز أشرب
tired (adj)	ta‘bān	تعبان
to be worried	’ele’	قلق
to be nervous	etwattar	إتوتّر

hope	amal (m)	أمل
to hope (vi, vt)	tamanna	تمنّى
character	ʃaχṣiya (f)	شخصية
modest (adj)	motawāḍe'	متواضع
lazy (adj)	kaslān	كسلان
generous (adj)	karīm	كريم
talented (adj)	mawhūb	موهوب
honest (adj)	amīn	أمين
serious (adj)	gād	جاد
shy, timid (adj)	χagūl	خجول
sincere (adj)	moχleṣ	مخلص
coward	gabān (m)	جبان
to sleep (vi)	nām	نام
dream	ḥelm (m)	حلم
bed	serīr (m)	سرير
pillow	maχadda (f)	مخدّة
insomnia	araq (m)	أرق
to go to bed	rāḥ lel serīr	راح للسرير
nightmare	kabūs (m)	كابوس
alarm clock	monabbeh (m)	منبّه
smile	ebtesāma (f)	إبتسامة
to smile (vi)	ebtasam	إبتسم
to laugh (vi)	ḍeḥek	ضحك
quarrel	χenā'a (f)	خناقة
insult	ehāna (f)	إهانة
resentment	esteyā' (m)	إستياء
angry (mad)	ɣaḍbān	غضبان

7. Clothing. Personal accessories

clothes	malābes (pl)	ملابس
coat (overcoat)	balṭo (m)	بالطو
fur coat	balṭo farww (m)	بالطو فروّ
jacket (e.g., leather ~)	ʒæket (m)	جاكيت
raincoat (trenchcoat, etc.)	ʒæket lel maṭar (m)	جاكيت للمطر
shirt (button shirt)	'amīṣ (m)	قميص
pants	banṭalone (f)	بنطلون
suit jacket	ʒæket (f)	جاكت
suit	badla (f)	بدلة
dress (frock)	fostān (m)	فستان
skirt	ʒība (f)	جيبة
T-shirt	ti ʃirt (m)	تي شيرت

bathrobe	robe el ḥammām (m)	روب حمّام
pajamas	beʒāma (f)	بيجاما
workwear	lebs el ʃoɣl (m)	لبس الشغل
underwear	malābes dāχeliya (pl)	ملابس داخلية
socks	ʃarāb (m)	شراب
bra	setyāna (f)	ستيانة
pantyhose	klone (m)	كلون
stockings (thigh highs)	gawāreb (pl)	جوارب
bathing suit	mayo (m)	مايّوه
hat	ṭa'iya (f)	طاقيّة
footwear	gezam (pl)	جزم
boots (e.g., cowboy ~)	būt (m)	بوت
heel	ka'b (m)	كعب
shoestring	ʃerī'ṭ (m)	شريط
shoe polish	warnīʃ el gazma (m)	ورنيش الجزمة
cotton (n)	'oṭn (m)	قطن
wool (n)	ṣūf (m)	صوف
fur (n)	farww (m)	فروّ
gloves	gwanty (m)	جوانتي
mittens	gwanty men ɣeyr aṣābe' (m)	جوانتي من غير أصابع
scarf (muffler)	skarf (m)	سكارف
glasses (eyeglasses)	naḍḍāra (f)	نظّارة
umbrella	ʃamsiya (f)	شمسيّة
tie (necktie)	karavetta (f)	كرافتة
handkerchief	mandīl (m)	منديل
comb	meʃṭ (m)	مشط
hairbrush	forʃet ʃa'r (f)	فرشة شعر
buckle	bokla (f)	بكلة
belt	ḥezām (m)	حزام
purse	ʃanṭet yad (f)	شنطة يد
collar	yā'a (f)	ياقة
pocket	geyb (m)	جيب
sleeve	komm (m)	كمّ
fly (on trousers)	lesān (m)	لسان
zipper (fastener)	sosta (f)	سوستة
button	zerr (m)	زرّ
to get dirty (vi)	ettwassaχ	إتوّسّخ
stain (mark, spot)	bo''a (f)	بقعة

8. City. Urban institutions

store	maḥal (m)	محل
shopping mall	mole (m)	مول

supermarket	subermarket (m)	سوبرماركت
shoe store	maḥal gezam (m)	محل جزم
bookstore	maḥal kotob (m)	محل كتب
drugstore, pharmacy	ṣaydaliya (f)	صيدليّة
bakery	maχbaz (m)	مخبز
pastry shop	ḥalawāny (m)	حلواني
grocery store	ba''āla (f)	بقّالة
butcher shop	gezāra (f)	جزارة
produce store	dokkān χoḍār (m)	دكّان خضار
market	sūʾ (f)	سوق
hair salon	ṣalone ḥelāʾa (m)	صالون حلاقة
post office	maktab el barīd (m)	مكتب البريد
dry cleaners	dray klīn (m)	دراي كلين
circus	serk (m)	سيرك
zoo	ḥadīqet el ḥayawān (f)	حديقة حيوان
theater	masraḥ (m)	مسرح
movie theater	sinema (f)	سينما
museum	mat-ḥaf (m)	متحف
library	maktaba (f)	مكتبة
mosque	masged (m)	مسجد
synagogue	kenīs (m)	كنيس
cathedral	katedraʾiya (f)	كاتدرائية
temple	maʿbad (m)	معبد
church	kenīsa (f)	كنيسة
college	kolliya (m)	كليّة
university	gamʿa (f)	جامعة
school	madrasa (f)	مدرسة
hotel	fondoʾ (m)	فندق
bank	bank (m)	بنك
embassy	safāra (f)	سفارة
travel agency	ʃerket seyāḥa (f)	شركة سياحة
subway	metro (m)	مترو
hospital	mostaʃfa (m)	مستشفى
gas station	maḥaṭṭet banzīn (f)	محطّة بنزين
parking lot	mawʾef el ʿarabeyāt (m)	موقف العربيات
ENTRANCE	doχūl	دخول
EXIT	χorūg	خروج
PUSH	edfaʿ	إدفع
PULL	es-ḥab	إسحب
OPEN	maftūḥ	مفتوح
CLOSED	moɣlaq	مغلق
monument	temsāl (m)	تمثال
fortress	ʾalʿa (f)	قلعة

palace	'aṣr (m)	قصر
medieval (adj)	men el qorūn el wosṭa	من القرون الوسطى
ancient (adj)	'atīq	عتيق
national (adj)	waṭany	وطني
famous (monument, etc.)	maʃ-hūr	مشهور

9. Money. Finances

money	folūs (pl)	فلوس
coin	'erʃ (m)	قرش
dollar	dolār (m)	دولار
euro	yoro (m)	يورو
ATM	makinet ṣarrāf 'āly (f)	ماكينة صرّاف آلي
currency exchange	ṣarrāfa (f)	صرّافة
exchange rate	se'r el ṣarf (m)	سعر الصرف
cash	kæʃ (m)	كاش
How much?	bekām?	بكام؟
to pay (vi, vt)	dafa'	دفع
payment	daf' (m)	دفع
change (give the ~)	el bā'y (m)	الباقي
price	se'r (m)	سعر
discount	χaṣm (m)	خصم
cheap (adj)	reχīṣ	رخيص
expensive (adj)	ɣāly	غالي
bank	bank (m)	بنك
account	ḥesāb (m)	حساب
credit card	kredit kard (f)	كريدت كارد
check	ʃīk (m)	شيك
to write a check	katab ʃīk	كتب شيك
checkbook	daftar ʃikāt (m)	دفتر شيكات
debt	deyn (m)	دين
debtor	modīn (m)	مدين
to lend (money)	sallef	سلّف
to borrow (vi, vt)	estalaf	إستلف
to rent (~ a tuxedo)	est'gar	إستأجر
on credit (adv)	bel ta'seeṭ	بالتقسيط
wallet	maḥfaẓa (f)	محفظة
safe	χazzāna (f)	خزّانة
inheritance	werāsa (f)	وراثة
fortune (wealth)	sarwa (f)	ثروّة
tax	ḍarība (f)	ضريبة
fine	ɣarāma (f)	غرامة
to fine (vt)	faraḍ ɣarāma	فرض غرامة

wholesale (adj)	el gomla	الجملة
retail (adj)	yebee‘ bel tagze’a	يبيع بالتجزئة
to insure (vt)	ammen	أمّن
insurance	ta’mīn (m)	تأمين
capital	ra’s māl (m)	رأس مال
turnover	dawret ra’s el māl (f)	دورة رأس المال
stock (share)	sahm (m)	سهم
profit	rebḥ (m)	ربح
profitable (adj)	morbeḥ	مربح
crisis	azma (f)	أزمة
bankruptcy	eflās (m)	إفلاس
to go bankrupt	falles	فلّس
accountant	muḥāseb (m)	محاسب
salary	morattab (m)	مرتّب
bonus (money)	‘alāwa (f)	علاوة

10. Transportation

bus	buṣ (m)	باص
streetcar	trām (m)	ترام
trolley bus	trolly buṣ (m)	ترولي باص
to go by ...	rāḥ be ...	راح بـ ...
to get on (~ the bus)	rekeb	ركب
to get off ...	nezel men	نزل من
stop (e.g., bus ~)	maw’af (m)	موّقف
terminus	’āχer maw’af (m)	آخر موقف
schedule	gadwal (m)	جدوّل
ticket	tazkara (f)	تذكرة
to be late (for ...)	met’akχer	متأخّر
taxi, cab	taksi (m)	تاكسي
by taxi	bel taksi	بالتاكسي
taxi stand	maw’ef taksi (m)	موّقف تاكسي
traffic	ḥaraket el morūr (f)	حركة المرور
rush hour	sā‘et el zorwa (f)	ساعة الذروة
to park (vi)	rakan	ركن
subway	metro (m)	مترو
station	maḥaṭṭa (f)	محطّة
train	qeṭār, ’aṭṭr (m)	قطار
train station	maḥaṭṭet qeṭār (f)	محطّة قطار
rails	qoḍbān (pl)	قضبان
compartment	ɣorfa (f)	غرفة
berth	serīr (m)	سرير

airplane	ṭayāra (f)	طيّارة
air ticket	tazkara ṭayarān (f)	تذكرة طيران
airline	ʃerket ṭayarān (f)	شركة طيران
airport	maṭār (m)	مطار
flight (act of flying)	ṭayarān (m)	طيران
luggage	el ʃonaṭ (pl)	الشنط
luggage cart	'arabet ʃonaṭ (f)	عربة شنط
ship	safīna (f)	سفينة
cruise ship	safīna seyaḥiya (f)	سفينة سياحيّة
yacht	yaχt (m)	يخت
boat (flat-bottomed ~)	markeb (m)	مركب
captain	'obṭān (m)	قبطان
cabin	kabīna (f)	كابينة
port (harbor)	minā' (m)	ميناء
bicycle	beskeletta (f)	بيسكلتّة
scooter	fezba (f)	فزبة
motorcycle, bike	motosekl (m)	موتوسيكل
pedal	dawwāsa (f)	دوّاسة
pump	ṭolommba (f)	طلمبّة
wheel	'agala (f)	عجلة
automobile, car	sayāra (f)	سيّارة
ambulance	es'āf (m)	إسعاف
truck	ʃāḥena (f)	شاحنة
used (adj)	mosta'mal	مستعمل
car crash	ḥadset sayāra (f)	حادثة سيارة
repair	taṣlīḥ (m)	تصليح

11. Food. Part 1

meat	laḥma (f)	لحمة
chicken	ferāχ (m)	فراخ
duck	baṭṭa (f)	بطّة
pork	laḥm el χanazīr (m)	لحم الخنزير
veal	laḥm el 'egl (m)	لحم العجل
lamb	laḥm ḍāny (m)	لحم ضاني
beef	laḥm baqary (m)	لحم بقري
sausage (bologna, pepperoni, etc.)	sogo'' (m)	سجق
egg	beyḍa (f)	بيضة
fish	samak (m)	سمك
cheese	gebna (f)	جبنة
sugar	sokkar (m)	سكّر
salt	melḥ (m)	ملح

rice	rozz (m)	رزّ
pasta (macaroni)	makaruna (f)	مكرونة
butter	zebda (f)	زبدة
vegetable oil	zeyt (m)	زيت
bread	‘eyʃ (m)	عيش
chocolate (n)	ʃokolāta (f)	شكولاتة
wine	χamra (f)	خمرة
coffee	’ahwa (f)	قهوة
milk	laban (m)	لبن
juice	‘aṣīr (m)	عصير
beer	bīra (f)	بيرة
tea	ʃāy (m)	شاي
tomato	ṭamāṭem (f)	طماطم
cucumber	χeyār (m)	خيار
carrot	gazar (m)	جزر
potato	baṭāṭes (f)	بطاطس
onion	baṣal (m)	بصل
garlic	tūm (m)	ثوم
cabbage	koronb (m)	كرنب
beetroot	bangar (m)	بنجر
eggplant	bātengān (m)	باذنجان
dill	ʃabat (m)	شبت
lettuce	χass (m)	خسّ
corn (maize)	dora (f)	ذرة
fruit	faχa (f)	فاكهة
apple	toffāḥa (f)	تفّاحة
pear	komettra (f)	كمّثرى
lemon	lymūn (m)	ليمون
orange	bortoqāl (m)	برتقال
strawberry (garden ~)	farawla (f)	فراولة
plum	bar’ū’ (m)	برقوق
raspberry	tūt el ‘alī’ el aḥmar (m)	توت العليق الأحمر
pineapple	ananās (m)	أناناس
banana	moze (m)	موز
watermelon	baṭṭīχ (m)	بطّيخ
grape	‘enab (m)	عنب
melon	ʃammām (f)	شمّام

12. Food. Part 2

cuisine	maṭbaχ (m)	مطبخ
recipe	waṣfa (f)	وصفة
food	akl (m)	أكل
to have breakfast	feṭer	فطر
to have lunch	etɣadda	إتغدّى

to have dinner	etʿasʃa	إتعشّى
taste, flavor	ṭaʿm (m)	طعم
tasty (adj)	ḥelw	حلو
cold (adj)	bāred	بارد
hot (adj)	soχn	سخن
sweet (sugary)	mesakkar	مسكّر
salty (adj)	māleḥ	مالح
sandwich (bread)	sandawitʃ (m)	ساندويتش
side dish	ṭabaʾ gāneby (m)	طبق جانبي
filling (for cake, pie)	ḥaʃwa (f)	حشوة
sauce	ṣalṣa (f)	صلصة
piece (of cake, pie)	ʾeṭʿa (f)	قطعة
diet	reʒīm (m)	رجيم
vitamin	vitamīn (m)	فيتامين
calorie	soʿra ḥarāriya (f)	سعرة حراريّة
vegetarian (n)	nabāty (m)	نباتي
restaurant	maṭʿam (m)	مطعم
coffee house	ʾahwa (f), kaféih (m)	قهوة ,كافيه
appetite	ʃahiya (f)	شهيّة
Enjoy your meal!	bel hana wel ʃefa!	بالهنا والشفا!
waiter	garsone (m)	جرسون
waitress	garsona (f)	جرسونة
bartender	bārman (m)	بارمان
menu	qāʾemet el ṭaʿām (f)	قائمة طعام
spoon	maʿlaʾa (f)	معلقة
knife	sekkīna (f)	سكّينة
fork	ʃawka (f)	شوكة
cup (e.g., coffee ~)	fengān (m)	فنجان
plate (dinner ~)	ṭabaʾ (m)	طبق
saucer	ṭabaʾ fengān (m)	طبق فنجان
napkin (on table)	mandīl waraʾ (m)	منديل ورق
toothpick	χallet senān (f)	خلة سنان
to order (meal)	ṭalab	طلب
course, dish	wagba (f)	وجبة
portion	naṣīb (m)	نصيب
appetizer	moqabbelāt (pl)	مقبّلات
salad	solṭa (f)	سلطة
soup	ʃorba (f)	شوربة
dessert	ḥalawīāt (pl)	حلويّات
jam (whole fruit jam)	mrabba (m)	مربّى
ice-cream	ʾays krīm (m)	آيس كريم
check	ḥesāb (m)	حساب
to pay the check	dafaʿ el ḥesāb	دفع الحساب
tip	baʾʃīʃ (m)	بقشيش

13. House. Apartment. Part 1

house	beyt (m)	بيت
country house	villa rīfiya (f)	فيلا ريفيّة
villa (seaside ~)	villa (f)	فيلا
floor, story	dore (m)	دور
entrance	madχal (m)	مدخل
wall	ḥeyṭa (f)	حيطة
roof	sa'f (m)	سقف
chimney	madχana (f)	مدخنة
attic (storage place)	'elya (f)	علية
window	ʃebbāk (m)	شبّاك
window ledge	ḥāfet el ʃebbāk (f)	حافة الشبّاك
balcony	balakona (f)	بلكونة
stairs (stairway)	sellem (m)	سلّم
mailbox	ṣandū' el barīd (m)	صندوق البريد
garbage can	ṣandū' el zebāla (m)	صندوق الزبالة
elevator	asanseyr (m)	اسانسير
electricity	kahraba' (m)	كهرباء
light bulb	lammba (f)	لمّبة
switch	meftāḥ (m)	مفتاح
wall socket	bareza el kaharaba' (f)	بريزة الكهرباء
fuse	fetīl (m)	فتيل
door	bāb (m)	باب
handle, doorknob	okret el bāb (f)	اوكرة الباب
key	meftāḥ (m)	مفتاح
doormat	seggādet bāb (f)	سجّادة باب
door lock	'efl el bāb (m)	قفل الباب
doorbell	garas (m)	جرس
knock (at the door)	ṭar', da'' (m)	طرق, دقّ
to knock (vi)	χabbaṭ	خبّط
peephole	el 'eyn el seḥriya (m)	العين السحرية
yard	sāḥa (f)	ساحة
garden	geneyna (f)	جنينة
swimming pool	ḥammām sebāḥa (m)	حمّام سباحة
gym (home gym)	gīm (m)	جيم
tennis court	mal'ab tennis (m)	ملعب تنس
garage	garāʒ (m)	جراج
private property	melkiya χāṣa (f)	ملكيّة خاصّة
warning sign	lāfetat taḥzīr (f)	لافتة تحذير
security	ḥerāsa (f)	حراسة
security guard	ḥāres amn (m)	حارس أمن
renovations	tagdīdāt (m)	تجديدات
to renovate (vt)	gadded	جدّد

to put in order	nazzam	نظّم
to paint (~ a wall)	dahhen	دهّن
wallpaper	wara' ḥā'eṭ (m)	ورق حائط
to varnish (vt)	ṭala bel warnīʃ	طلى بالورنيش
pipe	masūra (f)	ماسورة
tools	adawāt (pl)	أدوات
basement	badrome (m)	بدروم
sewerage (system)	ʃabaket el magāry (f)	شبكة المجاري

14. House. Apartment. Part 2

apartment	ʃa''a (f)	شقّة
room	oḍa (f)	أوضة
bedroom	oḍet el nome (f)	أوضة النوم
dining room	oḍet el sofra (f)	أوضة السفرة
living room	oḍet el esteqbāl (f)	أوضة الإستقبال
study (home office)	maktab (m)	مكتب
entry room	madχal (m)	مدخل
bathroom (room with a bath or shower)	ḥammām (m)	حمّام
half bath	ḥammām (m)	حمّام
floor	arḍiya (f)	أرضية
ceiling	sa'f (m)	سقف
to dust (vt)	masaḥ el ɣobār	مسح الغبار
vacuum cleaner	maknasa kahraba'iya (f)	مكنسة كهربائيّة
to vacuum (vt)	naḍḍaf be maknasa kahrabā'iya	نظّف بمكنسة كهربائيّة
mop	ʃarʃūba (f)	شرشوبة
dust cloth	mamsaḥa (f)	ممسحة
short broom	ma'sʃa (f)	مقشّة
dustpan	lammāma (f)	لمّامة
furniture	asās (m)	أثاث
table	maktab (m)	مكتب
chair	korsy (m)	كرسي
armchair	korsy (m)	كرسي
bookcase	χazzānet kotob (f)	خزّانة كتب
shelf	raff (m)	رفّ
wardrobe	dolāb (m)	دولاب
mirror	merāya (f)	مراية
carpet	seggāda (f)	سجّادة
fireplace	daffāya (f)	دفّاية
drapes	satā'er (pl)	ستائر

table lamp	abāʒūr (f)	اباجورة
chandelier	nagafa (f)	نجفة
kitchen	maṭbaχ (m)	مطبخ
gas stove (range)	botoɣāz (m)	بوتوغاز
electric stove	forn kaharabā'y (m)	فرن كهربائي
microwave oven	mikroweyv (m)	ميكروويف
refrigerator	tallāga (f)	ثلاجة
freezer	freyzer (m)	فريزر
dishwasher	ɣassālet aṭbā' (f)	غسّالة أطباق
faucet	ḥanafiya (f)	حنفيّة
meat grinder	farrāmet laḥm (f)	فرّامة لحم
juicer	'aṣṣāra (f)	عصّارة
toaster	maḥmaṣet χobz (f)	محمصة خبز
mixer	χallāṭ (m)	خلّاط
coffee machine	makinet ṣon' el 'ahwa (f)	ماكينة صنع القهوة
kettle	ɣallāya (f)	غلّاية
teapot	barrād el ʃāy (m)	برّاد الشاي
TV set	televizion (m)	تليفزيون
VCR (video recorder)	'āla tasgīl video (f)	آلة تسجيل فيديو
iron (e.g., steam ~)	makwa (f)	مكواة
telephone	telefon (m)	تليفون

15. Professions. Social status

director	modīr (m)	مدير
superior	motafawweq (m)	متفوّق
president	ra'īs (m)	رئيس
assistant	mosā'ed (m)	مساعد
secretary	sekerteyr (m)	سكرتير
owner, proprietor	ṣāḥeb (m)	صاحب
partner	ʃerīk (m)	شريك
stockholder	mālek el as-hom (m)	مالك الأسهم
businessman	ragol a'māl (m)	رجل أعمال
millionaire	millyonīr (m)	مليونير
billionaire	milliardīr (m)	مليارديـر
actor	momassel (m)	ممثّل
architect	mohandes me'māry (m)	مهندس معماري
banker	ṣāḥeb maṣraf (m)	صاحب مصرف
broker	semsār (m)	سمسار
veterinarian	doktore beṭary (m)	دكتور بيطري
doctor	doktore (m)	دكتور

chambermaid	ʿāmela tandīf ɣoraf (f)	عاملة تنظيف غرف
designer	moṣammem (m)	مصمّم
correspondent	morāsel (m)	مراسل
delivery man	rāgel el delivery (m)	راجل الديلفري
electrician	kahrabāʾy (m)	كهربائي
musician	ʿāzef (m)	عازف
babysitter	dāda (f)	دادة
hairdresser	ḥallāʾ (m)	حلاّق
herder, shepherd	rāʿy (m)	راعي
singer (masc.)	moṭreb (m)	مطرب
translator	motargem (m)	مترجم
writer	kāteb (m)	كاتب
carpenter	naggār (m)	نجّار
cook	ṭabbāχ (m)	طبّاخ
fireman	rāgel el maṭāfy (m)	راجل المطافئ
police officer	ʃorṭy (m)	شرطي
mailman	sāʿy el barīd (m)	ساعي البريد
programmer	mobarmeg (m)	مبرمج
salesman (store staff)	bayāʿ (m)	بيّاع
worker	ʿāmel (m)	عامل
gardener	bostāny (m)	بستاني
plumber	samkary (m)	سمكري
dentist	doktore asnān (m)	دكتور أسنان
flight attendant (fem.)	moḍīfet ṭayarān (f)	مضيفة طيران
dancer (masc.)	rāqeṣ (m)	راقص
bodyguard	ḥāres ʃaχṣy (m)	حارس شخصي
scientist	ʿālem (m)	عالِم
schoolteacher	modarres madrasa (m)	مدرس مدرسة
farmer	mozāreʿ (m)	مزارع
surgeon	garrāḥ (m)	جرّاح
miner	ʿāmel mangam (m)	عامل منجم
chef (kitchen chef)	el ʃeyf (m)	الشيف
driver	sawwāʾ (m)	سوّاق

16. Sport

kind of sports	nūʿ men el reyāḍa (m)	نوع من الرياضة
soccer	koret el qadam (f)	كرة القدم
hockey	hoky (m)	هوكي
basketball	koret el salla (f)	كرة السلّة
baseball	baseball (m)	بيسبول
volleyball	voliball (m)	فولي بول
boxing	molakma (f)	ملاكمة

wrestling	moṣar'a (f)	مصارعة
tennis	tennis (m)	تنس
swimming	sebāḥa (f)	سباحة
chess	ʃaṭarang (m)	شطرنج
running	garyī (m)	جري
athletics	al'āb el qowa (pl)	ألعاب القوى
figure skating	tazallog fanny 'alal galīd (m)	تزلّج فنّي على الجليد
cycling	rokūb el darragāt (m)	ركوب الدرّاجات
billiards	bilyardo (m)	بلياردو
bodybuilding	body building (m)	بادي بيلدنج
golf	golf (m)	جولف
scuba diving	ɣoṣe (m)	غوص
sailing	reyāḍa ebḥār el marākeb (f)	رياضة إبحار المراكب
archery	remāya (f)	رماية
period, half	ʃoṭe (m)	شوط
half-time	beyn el ʃoṭeyn	بين الشوطين
tie	ta'ādol (m)	تعادل
to tie (vi)	ta'ādal	تعادل
treadmill	trīdmil (f)	تريد ميل
player	lā'eb (m)	لاعب
substitute	lā'eb eḥteyāṭy (m)	لاعب إحتياطي
substitutes bench	dekket el eḥṭiāṭy (f)	دكّة الإحتياطي
match	mobarā (f)	مباراة
goal	marma (m)	مرمى
goalkeeper	ḥāres el marma (m)	حارس المرمى
goal (score)	hadaf (m)	هدف
Olympic Games	al'āb olombiya (pl)	ألعاب أولمبيّة
to set a record	fāz be raqam qeyāsy	فاز برقم قياسي
final	mobarāh neha'iya (f)	مباراة نهائيّة
champion	baṭal (m)	بطل
championship	boṭūla (f)	بطولة
winner	fā'ez (m)	فائز
victory	foze (m)	فوز
to win (vi)	fāz	فاز
to lose (not win)	χeser	خسر
medal	medalya (f)	ميدالية
first place	el martaba el ūla (f)	المرتبة الأولى
second place	el martaba el tanya (f)	المرتبة الثانية
third place	el martaba el talta (f)	المرتبة الثالثة
stadium	mal'ab (m)	ملعب
fan, supporter	moʃagge' (m)	مشجّع
trainer, coach	modarreb (m)	مدرّب
training	tadrīb (m)	تدريب

17. Foreign languages. Orthography

language	loɣa (f)	لغة
to study (vt)	daras	درس
pronunciation	noṭ' (m)	نطق
accent	lahga (f)	لهجة
noun	esm (m)	اسم
adjective	ṣefa (f)	صفة
verb	fe'l (m)	فعل
adverb	ẓarf (m)	ظرف
pronoun	ḍamīr (m)	ضمير
interjection	oslūb el ta'aggob (m)	أسلوب التعجّب
preposition	ḥarf el garr (m)	حرف الجرّ
root	gezr el kelma (m)	جذر الكلمة
ending	nehāya (f)	نهاية
prefix	sabaeqa (f)	سابقة
syllable	maqṭa' lafzy (m)	مقطع لفظي
suffix	lāḥeqa (f)	لاحقة
stress mark	nabra (f)	نبرة
period, dot	no'ṭa (f)	نقطة
comma	faṣla (f)	فاصلة
colon	no'ṭeteyn (pl)	نقطتين
ellipsis	talat no'aṭ (pl)	ثلاث نقط
question	so'āl (m)	سؤال
question mark	'alāmet estefhām (f)	علامة إستفهام
exclamation point	'alāmet ta'aggob (f)	علامة تعجّب
in quotation marks	beyn 'alamaty el eqtebās	بين علامتي الاقتباس
in parenthesis	beyn el qoseyn	بين القوسين
letter	ḥarf (m)	حرف
capital letter	ḥarf kebīr (m)	حرف كبير
sentence	gomla (f)	جملة
group of words	magmū'a men el kelamāt (pl)	مجموعة من الكلمات
expression	moṣṭalaḥ (m)	مصطلح
subject	fā'el (m)	فاعل
predicate	mosnad (m)	مسند
line	saṭr (m)	سطر
paragraph	faqra (f)	فقرة
synonym	morādef (m)	مرادف
antonym	motaḍād loɣawy (m)	متضاد لغوي
exception	estesnā' (m)	إستثناء
to underline (vt)	ḥaṭṭ xaṭṭ taḥt	حطّ خطّ تحت

rules	qawāʿed (pl)	قواعد
grammar	el naḥw wel ṣarf (m)	النحو والصرف
vocabulary	mofradāt el loɣa (pl)	مفردات اللغة
phonetics	ṣawtīāt (pl)	صوتيات
alphabet	abgadiya (f)	أبجدية
textbook	ketāb taʿlīm (m)	كتاب تعليم
dictionary	qamūs (m)	قاموس
phrasebook	ketāb lel ʿebarāt el ʃāʾeʿa (m)	كتاب للعبارت الشائعة
word	kelma (f)	كلمة
meaning	maʿna (m)	معنى
memory	zākera (f)	ذاكرة

18. The Earth. Geography

the Earth	el arḍ (f)	الأرض
the globe (the Earth)	el kora el arḍiya (f)	الكرة الأرضيّة
planet	kawwkab (m)	كوّكب
geography	goɣrafia (f)	جغرافيا
nature	ṭabeeʿa (f)	طبيعة
map	χarīṭa (f)	خريطة
atlas	aṭlas (m)	أطلس
in the north	fel ʃamāl	في الشمال
in the south	fel ganūb	في الجنوب
in the west	fel ɣarb	في الغرب
in the east	fel ʃarʾ	في الشرق
sea	baḥr (m)	بحر
ocean	moḥīṭ (m)	محيط
gulf (bay)	χalīg (m)	خليج
straits	maḍīq (m)	مضيق
continent (mainland)	qārra (f)	قارّة
island	gezīra (f)	جزيرة
peninsula	ʃebh gezeyra (f)	شبه جزيرة
archipelago	magmūʿet gozor (f)	مجموعة جزر
harbor	mināʾ (m)	ميناء
coral reef	ʃoʿāb morganiya (pl)	شعاب مرجانية
shore	sāḥel (m)	ساحل
coast	sāḥel (m)	ساحل
flow (flood tide)	tayār (m)	تيّار
ebb (ebb tide)	gozor (m)	جزر
latitude	ʿarḍ (m)	عرض
longitude	χaṭṭ ṭūl (m)	خطّ طول

parallel	motawāz (m)	متواز
equator	xaṭṭ el estewā' (m)	خطّ الإستواء
sky	samā' (f)	سماء
horizon	ofoq (m)	أفق
atmosphere	el ɣelāf el gawwy (m)	الغلاف الجوّي
mountain	gabal (m)	جبل
summit, top	qemma (f)	قمّة
cliff	garf (m)	جرف
hill	tall (m)	تلّ
volcano	borkān (m)	بركان
glacier	nahr galīdy (m)	نهر جليدي
waterfall	ʃallāl (m)	شلاّل
plain	sahl (m)	سهل
river	nahr (m)	نهر
spring (natural source)	'eyn (m)	عين
bank (of river)	ḍaffa (f)	ضفّة
downstream (adv)	ma' ettigāh magra el nahr	مع إتّجاه مجرى النهر
upstream (adv)	ḍed el tayār	ضد التيار
lake	boḥeyra (f)	بحيرة
dam	sadd (m)	سدّ
canal	qanah (f)	قناة
swamp (marshland)	mostanqa' (m)	مستنقع
ice	galīd (m)	جليد

19. Countries of the world. Part 1

Europe	orobba (f)	أوروبّا
European Union	el etteḥād el orobby (m)	الإتّحاد الأوروبّي
European (n)	orobby (m)	أوروبّي
European (adj)	orobby	أوروبي
Austria	el nemsa (f)	النمسا
Great Britain	briṭaniya el 'ozma (f)	بريطانيا العظمى
England	engeltera (f)	إنجلترا
Belgium	balʒīka (f)	بلجيكا
Germany	almānya (f)	ألمانيا
Netherlands	holanda (f)	هولندا
Holland	holanda (f)	هولندا
Greece	el yunān (f)	اليونان
Denmark	el denmark (f)	الدنمارك
Ireland	irelanda (f)	أيرلندا
Iceland	'āyslanda (f)	آيسلندا
Spain	asbānya (f)	إسبانيا

Italy	eṭālia (f)	إيطاليا
Cyprus	'obroṣ (f)	قبرص
Malta	malṭa (f)	مالطا
Norway	el nerwīg (f)	النرويج
Portugal	el bortoɣāl (f)	البرتغال
Finland	finlanda (f)	فنلندا
France	faransa (f)	فرنسا
Sweden	el sweyd (f)	السويد
Switzerland	swesra (f)	سويسرا
Scotland	oskotlanda (f)	اسكتلندا
Vatican	el vatikān (m)	الفاتيكان
Liechtenstein	liʃtenʃtayn (m)	ليشتنشتاين
Luxembourg	luksemburg (f)	لوكسمبورج
Monaco	monako (f)	موناكو
Albania	albānia (f)	ألبانيا
Bulgaria	bolɣāria (f)	بلغاريا
Hungary	el magar (f)	المجر
Latvia	latvia (f)	لاتفيا
Lithuania	litwānia (f)	ليتوانيا
Poland	bolanda (f)	بولندا
Romania	romānia (f)	رومانيا
Serbia	ṣerbia (f)	صربيا
Slovakia	slovākia (f)	سلوفاكيا
Croatia	kroātya (f)	كرواتيا
Czech Republic	gomhoriya el tʃīk (f)	جمهورية التشيك
Estonia	estūnia (f)	إستونيا
Bosnia and Herzegovina	el bosna wel harsek (f)	البوسنة والهرسك
Macedonia (Republic of ~)	maqdūnia (f)	مقدونيا
Slovenia	slovenia (f)	سلوفينيا
Montenegro	el gabal el aswad (m)	الجبل الأسوّد
Belarus	belarūsia (f)	بيلاروسيا
Moldova, Moldavia	moldāvia (f)	مولدافيا
Russia	rūsya (f)	روسيا
Ukraine	okrānia (f)	أوكرانيا

20. Countries of the world. Part 2

Asia	asya (f)	آسيا
Vietnam	vietnām (f)	فيتنام
India	el hend (f)	الهند
Israel	isra'īl (f)	إسرائيل
China	el ṣīn (f)	الصين
Lebanon	lebnān (f)	لبنان
Mongolia	manɣūlia (f)	منغوليا

Malaysia	malīzya (f)	ماليزيا
Pakistan	bakistān (f)	باكستان
Saudi Arabia	el soʿodiya (f)	السعوديّة
Thailand	tayland (f)	تايلاند
Taiwan	taywān (f)	تايوان
Turkey	turkia (f)	تركيا
Japan	el yabān (f)	اليابان
Afghanistan	afɣanistan (f)	أفغانستان
Bangladesh	bangladeʃ (f)	بنجلاديش
Indonesia	indonisya (f)	إندونيسيا
Jordan	el ordon (m)	الأردن
Iraq	el ʿerāq (m)	العراق
Iran	iran (f)	إيران
Cambodia	kambodya (f)	كمبوديا
Kuwait	el kuweyt (f)	الكويت
Laos	laos (f)	لاوس
Myanmar	myanmar (f)	ميانمار
Nepal	nebāl (f)	نيبال
United Arab Emirates	el emārāt el ʿarabiya el mottaḥeda (pl)	الإمارات العربية المتّحدة
Syria	soria (f)	سوريا
Palestine	felesṭīn (f)	فلسطين
South Korea	korea el ganūbiya (f)	كوريا الجنوبيّة
North Korea	korea el ʃamāliya (f)	كوريا الشماليّة
United States of America	el welayāt el mottaḥda el amrīkiya (pl)	الولايات المتّحدة الأمريكيّة
Canada	kanada (f)	كندا
Mexico	el maksīk (f)	المكسيك
Argentina	arʒantīn (f)	الأرجنتين
Brazil	el barazīl (f)	البرازيل
Colombia	kolombia (f)	كولومبيا
Cuba	kūba (f)	كوبا
Chile	tʃīly (f)	تشيلي
Venezuela	venzweyla (f)	فنزويلا
Ecuador	el equador (f)	الإكوادور
The Bahamas	gozor el bahāmas (pl)	جزر البهاماس
Panama	banama (f)	بنما
Egypt	maṣr (f)	مصر
Morocco	el maɣreb (m)	المغرب
Tunisia	tunis (f)	تونس
Kenya	kenya (f)	كينيا
Libya	libya (f)	ليبيا
South Africa	afreqia el ganūbiya (f)	أفريقيا الجنوبيّة
Australia	ostorālya (f)	أستراليا
New Zealand	nyu zelanda (f)	نيوزيلندا

21. Weather. Natural disasters

weather	ṭa's (m)	طقس
weather forecast	naʃra gawiya (f)	نشرة جويّة
temperature	ḥarāra (f)	حرارة
thermometer	termometr (m)	ترمومتر
barometer	barometr (m)	بارومتر
sun	ʃams (f)	شمس
to shine (vi)	nawwar	نوّر
sunny (day)	moʃmes	مشمس
to come up (vi)	ʃara'	شرق
to set (vi)	ɣarab	غرب
rain	maṭar (m)	مطر
it's raining	el donia betmaṭṭar	الدنيا بتمطّر
pouring rain	maṭar monhamer (f)	مطر منهمر
rain cloud	saḥābet maṭar (f)	سحابة مطر
puddle	berka (f)	بركة
to get wet (in rain)	ettbal	إتّبل
thunderstorm	'āṣefa ra'diya (f)	عاصفة رعدية
lightning (~ strike)	bar' (m)	برق
to flash (vi)	baraq	برق
thunder	ra'd (m)	رعد
it's thundering	el samā' dawat ra'd (f)	السماء دوّت رعد
hail	maṭar bard (m)	مطر برد
it's hailing	maṭṭaret bard	مطّرت برد
heat (extreme ~)	ḥarāra (f)	حرارة
it's hot	el gaww ḥarr	الجوّ حرّ
it's warm	el gaww dafa	الجوّ دفا
it's cold	el gaww bāred	الجوّ بارد
fog (mist)	ʃabbūra (f)	شبّورة
foggy	fih ʃabbūra	فيه شبّورة
cloud	saḥāba (f)	سحابة
cloudy (adj)	meɣayem	مغيّم
humidity	roṭūba (f)	رطوبة
snow	talg (m)	ثلج
it's snowing	fih talg	فيه ثلج
frost (severe ~, freezing cold)	ṣaqee' (m)	صقيع
below zero (adv)	taḥt el ṣefr	تحت الصفر
hoarfrost	ṣaqee' motagammed (m)	صقيع متجمّد
bad weather	ṭa's saye' (m)	طقس سئ
disaster	karsa (f)	كارثة
flood, inundation	fayaḍān (m)	فيضان
avalanche	enheyār talgy (m)	إنهيار ثلجي

earthquake	zelzāl (m)	زلزال
tremor, quake	hazza arḍiya (f)	هزّة أرضية
epicenter	markaz el zelzāl (m)	مركز الزلزال
eruption	sawarān (m)	ثوّران
lava	ḥomam borkāniya (pl)	حمم بركانية
twister, tornado	eʿṣār (m)	إعصار
hurricane	eʿṣār (m)	إعصار
tsunami	tsunāmy (m)	تسونامي
cyclone	eʿṣār (m)	إعصار

22. Animals. Part 1

animal	ḥayawān (m)	حيوان
predator	moftares (m)	مفترس
tiger	nemr (m)	نمر
lion	asad (m)	أسد
wolf	ze'b (m)	ذئب
fox	taʿlab (m)	ثعلب
jaguar	nemr amrīky (m)	نمر أمريكي
lynx	waʃaq (m)	وشق
coyote	qayūṭ (m)	قيوط
jackal	ebn 'āwy (m)	ابن آوى
hyena	ḍebʿ (m)	ضبع
squirrel	sengāb (m)	سنجاب
hedgehog	qonfoz (m)	قنفذ
rabbit	arnab (m)	أرنب
raccoon	rakūn (m)	راكون
hamster	hamster (m)	هامستر
mole	χold (m)	خلد
mouse	fār (m)	فأر
rat	gerz (m)	جرذ
bat	χoffāʃ (m)	خفّاش
beaver	qondos (m)	قندس
horse	ḥoṣān (m)	حصان
deer	ayl (m)	أيل
camel	gamal (m)	جمل
zebra	ḥomār waḥʃy (m)	حمار وحشي
whale	ḥūt (m)	حوت
seal	foqma (f)	فقمة
walrus	el kabʿ (m)	الكبع
dolphin	dolfīn (m)	دولفين
bear	dobb (m)	دبّ
monkey	'erd (m)	قرد

elephant	fīl (m)	فيل
rhinoceros	χartīt (m)	خرتيت
giraffe	zarāfa (f)	زرافة
hippopotamus	faras el nahr (m)	فرس النهر
kangaroo	kangarū (m)	كانجّارو
cat	'oṭṭa (f)	قطّة
dog	kalb (m)	كلب
cow	ba'ara (f)	بقرة
bull	sore (m)	ثور
sheep (ewe)	χarūf (f)	خروف
goat	me'za (f)	معزة
donkey	ḥomār (m)	حمار
pig, hog	χenzīr (m)	خنزير
hen (chicken)	farχa (f)	فرخة
rooster	dīk (m)	ديك
duck	baṭṭa (f)	بطّة
goose	wezza (f)	وزّة
turkey (hen)	dīk rūmy (m)	ديك رومي
sheepdog	kalb rā'y (m)	كلب رعي

23. Animals. Part 2

bird	ṭā'er (m)	طائر
pigeon	ḥamāma (f)	حمامة
sparrow	'aṣfūr dawri (m)	عصفور دوري
tit (great tit)	qarqaf (m)	قرقف
magpie	'a''a' (m)	عقعق
eagle	'eqāb (m)	عقاب
hawk	el bāz (m)	الباز
falcon	ṣa'r (m)	صقر
swan	el temm (m)	التّم
crane	karkiya (m)	كركية
stork	loqloq (m)	لقلق
parrot	babaɣā' (m)	ببغاء
peacock	ṭawūs (m)	طاووس
ostrich	na'āma (f)	نعامة
heron	belʃone (m)	بلشون
nightingale	'andalīb (m)	عندليب
swallow	el sonūnū (m)	السنونو
woodpecker	na'ār el χaʃab (m)	نقار الخشب
cuckoo	weqwāq (m)	وقواق
owl	būma (f)	بومة
penguin	beṭrīq (m)	بطريق

tuna	tuna (f)	تونة
trout	salamon mera''aṭ (m)	سلمون مرقّط
eel	ḥankalīs (m)	حنكليس
shark	'erʃ (m)	قرش
crab	kaboria (m)	كابوريا
jellyfish	'andīl el baḥr (m)	قنديل البحر
octopus	aχṭabūṭ (m)	أخطبوط
starfish	negmet el baḥr (f)	نجمة البحر
sea urchin	qonfoz el baḥr (m)	قنفذ البحر
seahorse	ḥoṣān el baḥr (m)	حصان البحر
shrimp	gammbary (m)	جمّبري
snake	te'bān (m)	ثعبان
viper	af'a (f)	أفعى
lizard	seḥliya (f)	سحليّة
iguana	eɣwana (f)	إغوانة
chameleon	ḥerbāya (f)	حرباية
scorpion	'a'rab (m)	عقرب
turtle	solḥefah (f)	سلحفاة
frog	ḍeffḍa' (m)	ضفدع
crocodile	temsāḥ (m)	تمساح
insect, bug	ḥaʃara (f)	حشرة
butterfly	farāʃa (f)	فراشة
ant	namla (f)	نملة
fly	debbāna (f)	دبّانة
mosquito	namūsa (f)	ناموسة
beetle	χonfesa (f)	خنفسة
bee	naḥla (f)	نحلة
spider	'ankabūt (m)	عنكبوت

24. Trees. Plants

tree	ʃagara (f)	شجرة
birch	batola (f)	بتولا
oak	ballūṭ (f)	بلّوط
linden tree	zayzafūn (f)	زيزفون
aspen	ḥūr rāgef	حور راجف
maple	qayqab (f)	قيقب
spruce	rateng (f)	راتينج
pine	ṣonober (f)	صنوبر
cedar	el orz (f)	الأرز
poplar	ḥūr (f)	حور
rowan	ɣobayrā' (f)	غبيراء

beech	el zān (f)	الزان
elm	derdar (f)	دردار
ash (tree)	marān (f)	مران
chestnut	kastanā' (f)	كستناء
palm tree	naχla (f)	نخلة
bush	ʃogeyra (f)	شجيرة
mushroom	feṭr (f)	فطر
poisonous mushroom	feṭr sām (m)	فطر سام
cep (Boletus edulis)	feṭr boleṭe ma'kūl (m)	فطر بوليط مأكول
russula	feṭr russula (m)	فطر روسولا
fly agaric	feṭr amanīt el ṭā'er (m)	فطر أمانيت الطائر
death cap	feṭr amanīt falusyāny el sām (m)	فطر أمانيت فالوسياني السام
flower	zahra (f)	زهرة
bouquet (of flowers)	bokeyh (f)	بوكيه
rose (flower)	warda (f)	وردة
tulip	tolīb (f)	توليب
carnation	'oronfol (m)	قرنفل
camomile	kamomile (f)	كاموميل
cactus	ṣabbār (m)	صبّار
lily of the valley	zanbaq el wādy (f)	زنبق الوادي
snowdrop	zahrat el laban (f)	زهرة اللبن
water lily	niloferiya (f)	نيلوفرية
greenhouse (tropical ~)	ṣoba (f)	صوبة
lawn	ʻoʃb aχḍar (m)	عشب أخضر
flowerbed	geneynet zohūr (f)	جنينة زهور
plant	nabāt (m)	نبات
grass	ʻoʃb (m)	عشب
leaf	wara'a (f)	ورقة
petal	wara'et el zahra (f)	ورقة الزهرة
stem	sāq (f)	ساق
young plant (shoot)	nabta saɣīra (f)	نبتة صغيرة
cereal crops	maḥaṣīl el ḥubūb (pl)	محاصيل الحبوب
wheat	'amḥ (m)	قمح
rye	ʃelm mazrūʻ (m)	شيلم مزروع
oats	ʃofān (m)	شوفان
millet	el deχn (m)	الدُخن
barley	ʃeʻīr (m)	شعير
corn	dora (f)	ذرة
rice	rozz (m)	رزّ

25. Various useful words

balance (of situation)	tawāzon (m)	توازن
base (basis)	asās (m)	أساس
beginning	bedāya (f)	بداية
category	fe'a (f)	فئة
choice	eχteyār (m)	إختيار
coincidence	ṣodfa (f)	صدفة
comparison	moqarna (f)	مقارنة
degree (extent, amount)	daraga (f)	درجة
development	tanmeya (f)	تنمية
difference	far' (m)	فرق
effect (e.g., of drugs)	ta'sīr (m)	تأثير
effort (exertion)	mag-hūd (m)	مجهود
element	'onṣor (m)	عنصر
example (illustration)	mesāl (m)	مثال
fact	ḥaʔīa (f)	حقيقة
help	mosa'da (f)	مساعدة
ideal	mesāl (m)	مثال
kind (sort, type)	nū' (m)	نوع
mistake, error	χaṭa' (m)	خطأ
moment	laḥza (f)	لحظة
obstacle	'aqaba (f)	عقبة
part (~ of sth)	goz' (m)	جزء
pause (break)	estrāḥa (f)	إستراحة
position	mawqef (m)	موّقف
problem	moʃkela (f)	مشكلة
process	'amaliya (f)	عمليّة
progress	ta'addom (m)	تقدّم
property (quality)	χaṣṣa (f)	خاصّة
reaction	radd fe'l (m)	ردّ فعل
risk	moχaṭra (f)	مخاطرة
secret	serr (m)	سرّ
series	selsela (f)	سلسلة
shape (outer form)	ʃakl (m)	شكل
situation	ḥāla (f), waḍ' (m)	حالة, وضع
solution	ḥall (m)	حلّ
standard (adj)	'ādy -qeyāsy	عادي, قياسي
stop (pause)	estrāḥa (f)	إستراحة
style	oslūb (m)	أسلوب
system	nezām (m)	نظام

table (chart)	gadwal (m)	جدوَل
tempo, rate	eqā' (m)	إيقاع
term (word, expression)	moṣṭalaḥ (m)	مصطلح
truth (e.g., moment of ~)	ḥa'ī'a (f)	حقيقة
turn (please wait your ~)	dore (m)	دور
urgent (adj)	mesta'gel	مستعجل
utility (usefulness)	manf'a (f)	منفعة
variant (alternative)	ʃakl moχtalef (m)	شكل مختلف
way (means, method)	ṭarī'a (f)	طريقة
zone	mante'a (f)	منطقة

26. Modifiers. Adjectives. Part 1

additional (adj)	eḍāfy	إضافي
ancient (~ civilization)	'adīm	قديم
artificial (adj)	ṣenā'y	صناعي
bad (adj)	weḥeʃ	وحش
beautiful (person)	gamīl	جميل
big (in size)	kebīr	كبير
bitter (taste)	morr	مرّ
blind (sightless)	a'ma	أعمى
central (adj)	markazy	مركزي
children's (adj)	lel aṭfāl	للأطفال
clandestine (secret)	serry	سرّي
clean (free from dirt)	neḍīf	نظيف
clever (smart)	zaky	ذكي
compatible (adj)	motawāfaq	متوافق
contented (satisfied)	rāḍy	راضي
dangerous (adj)	χaṭīr	خطير
dead (not alive)	mayet	ميّت
dense (fog, smoke)	kasīf	كثيف
difficult (decision)	ṣa'b	صعب
dirty (not clean)	weseχ	وسخ
easy (not difficult)	sahl	سهل
empty (glass, room)	χāly	خالي
exact (amount)	maẓbūṭ	مظبوط
excellent (adj)	momtāz	ممتاز
excessive (adj)	mofreṭ	مفرط
exterior (adj)	χāregy	خارجي
fast (quick)	saree'	سريع
fertile (land, soil)	χeṣb	خصب
fragile (china, glass)	qābel lel kasr	قابل للكسر
free (at no cost)	be balāʃ	ببلاش

fresh (~ water)	ʿazb	عذب
frozen (food)	mogammad	مجمّد
full (completely filled)	malyān	مليان
happy (adj)	saʿīd	سعيد
hard (not soft)	gāmed	جامد
huge (adj)	ḍaχm	ضخم
ill (sick, unwell)	ʿayān	عيّان
immobile (adj)	sābet	ثابت
important (adj)	mohemm	مهمّ
interior (adj)	dāχely	داخلي
last (e.g., ~ week)	māḍy	ماضي
last (final)	ʾāχer	آخر
left (e.g., ~ side)	el ʃemāl	الشمال
legal (legitimate)	qanūny	قانوني
light (in weight)	χafīf	خفيف
liquid (fluid)	sāʾel	سائل
long (e.g., ~ hair)	ṭawīl	طويل
loud (voice, etc.)	ʿāly	عالي
low (voice)	wāṭy	واطي

27. Modifiers. Adjectives. Part 2

main (principal)	raʾīsy	رئيسي
matt, matte	maṭfy	مطفي
mysterious (adj)	ɣāmeḍ	غامض
narrow (street, etc.)	ḍayeʾ	ضيّق
native (~ country)	aṣly	أصلي
negative (~ response)	salby	سلبي
new (adj)	gedīd	جديد
next (e.g., ~ week)	elly gayī	اللي جاي
normal (adj)	ʿādy	عادي
not difficult (adj)	meʃ ṣaʿb	مش صعب
obligatory (adj)	ḍarūry	ضروري
old (house)	ʾadīm	قديم
open (adj)	maftūḥ	مفتوح
opposite (adj)	moqābel	مقابل
ordinary (usual)	ʿādy	عادي
original (unusual)	aṣly	أصلي
personal (adj)	ʃaχṣy	شخصي
polite (adj)	moʾaddab	مؤدّب
poor (not rich)	faʾīr	فقير
possible (adj)	momken	ممكن
principal (main)	asāsy	أساسي

probable (adj)	moḥtamal	محتمل
prolonged (e.g., ~ applause)	momtad	ممتد
public (open to all)	ʿām	عام
rare (adj)	nāder	نادر
raw (uncooked)	nayī	نيّ
right (not left)	el yemīn	اليمين
ripe (fruit)	mestewy	مستوّي
risky (adj)	mogāzef	مجازف
sad (~ look)	zaʿlān	زعلان
second hand (adj)	mostaʿmal	مستعمل
shallow (water)	ḍaḥl	ضحل
sharp (blade, etc.)	ḥād	حاد
short (in length)	ʾaṣīr	قصير
similar (adj)	ʃabīh	شبيه
small (in size)	ṣoɣeyyir	صغيّر
smooth (surface)	amlas	أملس
soft (~ toys)	nāʿem	ناعم
solid (~ wall)	matīn	متين
sour (flavor, taste)	ḥāmeḍ	حامض
spacious (house, etc.)	wāseʿ	واسع
special (adj)	χāṣṣ	خاصّ
straight (line, road)	mostaqīm	مستقيم
strong (person)	ʾawy	قوّي
stupid (foolish)	ɣaby	غبي
superb, perfect (adj)	momtāz	ممتاز
sweet (sugary)	mesakkar	مسكّر
tan (adj)	asmar	أسمر
tasty (delicious)	ṭaʿmo ḥelw	طعمه حلو
unclear (adj)	meʃ wāḍeḥ	مش واضح

28. Verbs. Part 1

to accuse (vt)	ettaham	إتّهم
to agree (say yes)	ettafaʾ	إتّفق
to announce (vt)	aʿlan	أعلن
to answer (vi, vt)	gāwab	جاوب
to apologize (vi)	eʿtazar	إعتذر
to arrive (vi)	weṣel	وصل
to ask (~ oneself)	saʾal	سأل
to be absent	ɣāb	غاب
to be afraid	χāf	خاف
to be born	etwalad	إتولّد

to be in a hurry	mesta'gel	مستعجل
to beat (to hit)	ḍarab	ضرب
to begin (vt)	bada'	بدأ
to believe (in God)	aman	أمن
to belong to ...	χaṣṣ	خصّ
to break (split into pieces)	kasar	كسر
to build (vt)	bana	بنى
to buy (purchase)	eʃtara	إشترى
can (v aux)	'eder	قدر
can (v aux)	'eder	قدر
to cancel (call off)	alɣa	ألغى
to catch (vt)	mesek	مسك
to change (vt)	ɣayar	غيّر
to check (to examine)	eχtabar	إختبر
to choose (select)	eχtār	إختار
to clean up (tidy)	ratteb	رتّب
to close (vt)	'afal	قفل
to compare (vt)	qāran	قارن
to complain (vi, vt)	ʃaka	شكا
to confirm (vt)	akkad	أكّد
to congratulate (vt)	hanna	هنّأ
to cook (dinner)	ḥaḍḍar	حضّر
to copy (vt)	nasaχ	نسخ
to cost (vt)	kallef	كلّف
to count (add up)	'add	عدّ
to count on ...	e'tamad 'ala ...	...إعتمد على
to create (vt)	'amal	عمل
to cry (weep)	baka	بكى
to dance (vi, vt)	ra'aṣ	رقص
to deceive (vi, vt)	χada'	خدع
to decide (~ to do sth)	'arrar	قرّر
to delete (vt)	masaḥ	مسح
to demand (request firmly)	ṭāleb	طالب
to deny (vt)	ankar	أنكر
to depend on ...	e'tamad 'ala ...	...إعتمد على
to despise (vt)	eḥtaqar	إحتقر
to die (vi)	māt	مات
to dig (vt)	ḥafar	حفر
to disappear (vi)	eχtafa	إختفى
to discuss (vt)	nā'eʃ	ناقش
to disturb (vt)	az'ag	أزعج

29. Verbs. Part 2

to dive (vi)	ɣāṣ	غاص
to divorce (vi)	ṭalla'	طلّق
to do (vt)	'amal	عمل
to doubt (have doubts)	ʃakk fe	شكّ في
to drink (vi, vt)	ʃereb	شرب
to drop (let fall)	wa''a'	وقّع
to dry (clothes, hair)	gaffaf	جفّف
to eat (vi, vt)	akal	أكل
to end (~ a relationship)	anha	أنهى
to excuse (forgive)	'azar	عذر
to exist (vi)	kān mawgūd	كان موّجود
to expect (foresee)	tanabba'	تنبّأ
to explain (vt)	ʃaraḥ	شرح
to fall (vi)	we'e'	وقع
to fight (street fight, etc.)	χāne'	خانق
to find (vt)	la'a	لقى
to finish (vt)	χallaṣ	خلّص
to fly (vi)	ṭār	طار
to forbid (vt)	mana'	منع
to forget (vi, vt)	nesy	نسي
to forgive (vt)	'afa	عفا
to get tired	te'eb	تعب
to give (vt)	edda	إدّى
to go (on foot)	meʃy	مشى
to hate (vt)	kereh	كره
to have (vt)	malak	ملك
to have breakfast	feṭer	فطر
to have dinner	et'asʃa	إتعشّى
to have lunch	etɣadda	إتغدّى
to hear (vt)	seme'	سمع
to help (vt)	sā'ed	ساعد
to hide (vt)	χabba	خبّأ
to hope (vi, vt)	tamanna	تمنّى
to hunt (vi, vt)	eṣṭād	اصطاد
to hurry (vi)	esta'gel	إستعجل
to insist (vi, vt)	aṣarr	أصرّ
to insult (vt)	ahān	أهان
to invite (vt)	'azam	عزم
to joke (vi)	hazzar	هزّر
to keep (vt)	ḥafaẓ	حفظ
to kill (vt)	'atal	قتل
to know (sb)	'eref	عرف

to know (sth)	ʻeref	عرف
to like (I like ...)	ʻagab	عجب
to look at ...	baṣṣ	بصّ
to lose (umbrella, etc.)	ḍayaʻ	ضيّع
to love (sb)	ḥabb	حبّ
to make a mistake	ɣeleṭ	غلط
to meet (vi, vt)	ʼābel	قابل
to miss (school, etc.)	ɣāb	غاب

30. Verbs. Part 3

to obey (vi, vt)	ṭāʻ	طاع
to open (vt)	fataḥ	فتح
to participate (vi)	ʃārek	شارك
to pay (vi, vt)	dafaʻ	دفع
to permit (vt)	samaḥ	سمح
to play (children)	leʻeb	لعب
to pray (vi, vt)	ṣalla	صلّى
to promise (vt)	waʻad	وعد
to propose (vt)	ʻaraḍ	عرض
to prove (vt)	asbat	أثبت
to read (vi, vt)	ʼara	قرأ
to receive (vt)	estalam	إستلم
to rent (sth from sb)	estʼgar	إستأجر
to repeat (say again)	karrar	كرّر
to reserve, to book	ḥagaz	حجز
to run (vi)	gery	جري
to save (rescue)	anqaz	أنقذ
to say (~ thank you)	ʼāl	قال
to see (vt)	ʃāf	شاف
to sell (vt)	bāʻ	باع
to send (vt)	arsal	أرسل
to shoot (vi)	ḍarab bel nār	ضرب بالنار
to shout (vi)	ṣarraχ	صرّخ
to show (vt)	warra	ورّى
to sign (document)	waqqaʻ	وقّع
to sing (vi)	ɣanna	غنّى
to sit down (vi)	ʼaʻad	قعد
to smile (vi)	ebtasam	إبتسم
to speak (vi, vt)	kallem	كلّم
to steal (money, etc.)	saraʼ	سرق
to stop (please ~ calling me)	baṭṭal	بطّل
to study (vt)	daras	درس

to swim (vi)	'ām	عام
to take (vt)	aχad	أخد
to talk to ...	kallem ...	كلّم...
to tell (story, joke)	ḥaka	حكى
to thank (vt)	ʃakar	شكر
to think (vi, vt)	fakkar	فكّر
to translate (vt)	targem	ترجم
to trust (vt)	wasaq	وثق
to try (attempt)	ḥāwel	حاول
to turn (e.g., ~ left)	ḥād	حاد
to turn off	ṭaffa	طفّى
to turn on	fataḥ, ʃagɣal	فتح, شغّل
to understand (vt)	fehem	فهم
to wait (vt)	estanna	إستنّى
to want (wish, desire)	'āyez	عايز
to work (vi)	eʃtaɣal	إشتغل
to write (vt)	katab	كتب

www.ingramcontent.com/pod-product-compliance
Lightning Source LLC
Chambersburg PA
CBHW070115070426
42448CB00039B/2870
* 9 7 8 1 7 8 7 1 6 9 2 8 9 *